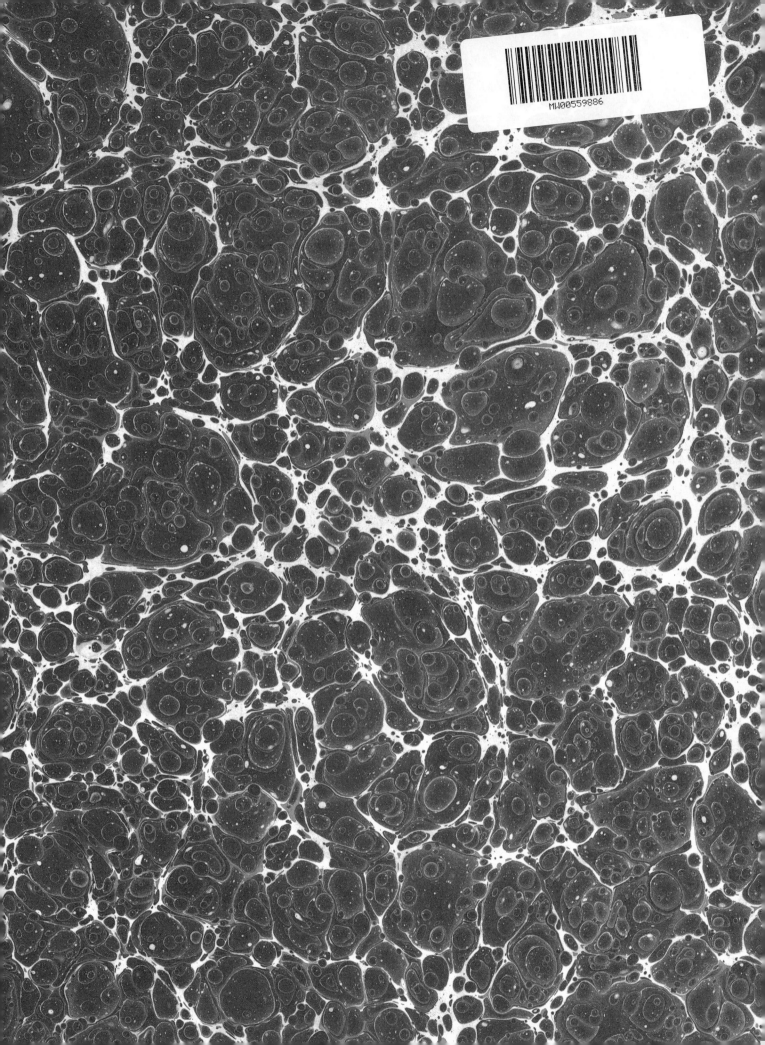

The Making of
Hunting Decoys

The Making of
Hunting Decoys

By William Veasey

Schiffer Publishing Ltd

West Chester, Pennsylvania 19380

Other books by the author

Bills and Feet: An Artisan's Handbook, with Sina Kurman
Waterfowl Carving, Blue Ribbon Techniques, with Cary Schuler Hull
Waterfowl Painting, Blue Ribbon Techniques
Power Tool Carving, Blue Ribbon Techniques
Burning and Texturing Methods, Blue Ribbon Techniques
Birds of Prey, Blue Ribbon Techniques
Blue Ribbon Pattern Series
I—Full Size Decorative Decoy Patterns
II—Miniature Decoy Patterns
III—Head Patterns
IV—Song Bird Patterns
V—Shore Bird Patterns
VI—Miniature Decorative Patterns
VII—Hunting Birds

Cover photo: "Testing the rig."

Copyright © 1986 by William Veasey.
Library of Congress Catalog Number: 86-62452.

Printed in the United States of America.
ISBN: 0-88740-073-6
Published by Schiffer Publishing Ltd.
1469 Morstein Road, West Chester, Pennsylvania 19380

This book may be purchased from the publisher.
Please include $1.50 postage.
Try your bookstore first.

Acknowledgments

I wish to thank each of the carvers who have done a project in this book and particularly Dan Brown, for his extra help in photographing and providing information about Cigar Daisey. A very special thanks to Tricia Veasey for her talent and her willingness to drop her own projects to help with mine, and thanks to Jim Dodd for allowing us to photograph the Veasey decoys in his collection.

Photo credit by Project

Carl Addison	— Carl Addison
Robert Biddle	— John Biddle
Dan Brown	— Dan Brown
Delbert "Cigar" Daisey	— Dan Brown
Paul Dobrowski	— Paul Dobrowski
Harold Haman	— Ned Mayne & Tricia Veasey
Charlie "Speed" Joiner	— Tricia Veasey
Ned Mayne	— Ned Mayne & Tricia Veasey
Terry McNulty	— Emil Williams
Frank Muller	— Tricia Veasey
Ralph Nocerino	— Ralph Nocerino
Roe "Duc-Man" Terry	— Roe "Duc-Man" Terry
William Veasey	— Tricia Veasey
Gilmore "Butch" Waggoner	— Fred Gillotti
Harry J. Waite	— Harry J. Waite & Tricia Veasey

Gallery of finished decoys and cover photo by Tricia Veasey

Introduction

It has been acknowledged that the decoy is the only true American folk art. Folk art in that it is both functional and artistic, American in that the Indians fashioned decoys before the white man set foot here.

In recent years there has been a great development in the decoy, simply because of the competitive shows. In preparing the list of participants for this book, I took care to include a cross section of very fine competition-grade hunting decoys and very serviceable gunning decoys. In the process, we have true world champions; Paul Dobrowski, Terry McNulty and Ralph Nocerino, each of these have won the Lem and Steve Shooting Stool contest at the World Championships in Ocean City, Maryland.

We have many cross-overs who do decorative and gunning birds, such as Carl Addison, Dan Brown, Roe Terry and myself. "Speed" Joiner, "Butch" Waggoner, Bob Biddle and Harold Haman make gunning birds. Ned Mayne won the first Delaware Duck Stamp competition and carves both gunning and decorative decoys. Frank Muller a fine decorative carver, but for hunting he makes the famous "Currituck" swans and geese. Harry Waite is a maverick, while Delbert "Cigar" Daisey is legendary.

Here are fifteen of the finest decoy makers in the world: one from New York, three from New Jersey, two from Pennsylvania, three from Delaware, four from Maryland, and two from Virginia. This area represents some of the finest waterfowl hunting country in the nation.

There will be criticism from some who will say that many of these decoys are too "fancy", and they probably are—in the strictest sense. However, today, when someone makes a gunning bird, it is for either his own hunting rig, competition or a collectable. In each case, the carver will make the decoy in a manner which pleases him. Many of those who have developed the skills will put more into the decoy than is necessary. This one factor, in fact, is what constitutes folk art and maintains the mystique which has evolved around decoys.

There are many of these projects which are simple, direct and to the point, as if to say there will be no "fancy" foolishness here. That, too, is welcome and very much a part of what I have tried to embody here.

In the final analysis, I believe there is room for all three of the above mentioned categories. Having projects in detail for all three categories, we hopefully give a much broader view of "how to", so the student may choose for himself the area most suited to his needs. As those needs change, we hope we will still be of help.

During the process of doing this book, I found a wonderful appreciation of nature in all the people participating. Some of them no longer hunt, for whatever reasons. None of them, however, is anti-hunting. They all share a great love for the outdoors and for the birds their decoys represent. Many times I have been so caught up in the conversations, stories and comradship that I totally forgot that I was working. In fact, no one else could have as good a job as mine. I have truly enjoyed working with these people. They have added a greater dimension to my life by sharing themselves. It is my hope that our efforts here will add significantly to the lives of those who choose to use this work.

Bill Veasey
1986

Dedication

This work is dedicated to two of the last great romantics of our times: Robert G. Biddle III and Dr. Marshal Sasser. In spite of the pressures of modern life they have always been themselves and willing to share with the rest of us that special gift.

Contents

Foreword

My first recollection of hunting decoys was as a boy in my father's old woodshed. His grand old decoys were all canvasbacks and blackheads and were all of the upper Cheasepeake type. His dad, my grandfather, had not been a hunter but his only sister, thirteen years older than he, had married Earl Armour of Northeast, Maryland and the Armours we all avid hunters. It was with them that my dad experienced the great days of bushwacking on the Susquehanna Flats that will probably never come again. I recall Uncle Earl's visits when I was about ten years old. He spoke in a deep, low voice and the subject was always canvasback shooting on the flats. I sat on our old woodbox and listened while chills ran up and down my spine. Thus began my love of duck hunting and the love and appreciation for decoys came shortly thereafter.

My father promised to start me hunting when I was 14. I don't know whether that was the Maryland state law at that time or if it was his own rule but there was no advancing the shedule despite my persistent attempts. Those last two years before my fourteenth birthday were the longest in my life. Almost everything I did related somehow to getting ready for the big day. It was during this time that I began making decoys. I used one of my father's old blocks, I think it was a Will Heverin can, and started making heads in a high school shop class. Most of the wood I used was picked up along the Elk River at Port Herman, Maryland. Some of my early decoys floated like a cork and some were so heavy that little more than the head stuck out of the water, but I was proud of them and they worked when that magic day in November came, my fourteenth birthday. I've continued to carve and collect decoys ever since.

Most carvers name one person who has had the greatest influence on their work and development. Mine is Norris E. Pratt, the all time grand master of handtools as far as I am concerned. Though I met him after I had been making decoys for several years, he is the one who taught me to use, care for, and sharpen tools. He used a bandsaw like he was scared to death of it but he handled every handtool like an artist. Mr. Pratt didn't have a "style" but he had a knowledge of tools and a talent for showing me how to carve into wood what I had in my mind and on my sketchpad. I spent many pleasant days in his shop in Kimblesville carving and listening to hunting and decoy tales.

At this point in time the concept of wildfowl decoys as an artform has been fairly well estabished and the decoy makers, past and present, identified as true artists. It is my hope that Bill Veasey's book will stimulate new artists to join the decoy fraternity and start turning out a few creations of their own.

Bob Biddle
1986

Carl Addison

Ring-Necked Duck

Carl Addison lives in Bear, Delaware, and carves and hunts as a hobby. Carl says, "As a hunter and person who loves nature studies, I always admired handmade and crafted nature related items. In 1974 I attended a local wildlife and decoy show where I saw, for the first time, how lifelike and far advanced carver's work had become. At that show I met my good friend, Bill Veasey. I went home wanting to carve decoys and thinking I could. WRONG!!

A year or so later I began class with Bill. He started me out simply and would only show me advanced methods as I was ready to handle them. That spring I entered the World Decoy Competition with a pair of redheads. I came away with a 1st and a 3rd. That win encouraged me to work harder. I studied with Bill for a couple years until Jay Polite opened his classes. Bill suggested I study under Jay to further my carving ability by gaining a different view point." Today Carl uses a blend of both techniques as a base for his own classes. He gives thanks to these two carvers and friends. He has progressed to the point of being a proficient carver and teacher in his own right.

Over the years Carl has won scores of ribbons in various competition grade classes in regional, national and international shows. He enjoys all types of wildfowl art but his appreciation of the working decoy as an artform builds with each piece he carves and uses while hunting. He hopes that this section about working birds will help you, as a carver, to also add to the art form.

"The ultimate decoys are corn, live birds, and an amplified recording. However, the local game warden or the feds might frown a little on their use. Next best thing is a good accurate decoy that rides well. Though there are times when blackened clorox or milk bottles will work, such as a stormy changeable day, the

decoy if rigged right will be the best legal bet.

Conditions should dictate the best way to rig. On big open water I like a big rig of standard size birds with over sized birds on the lead and trailing ends. This allows numbers to tantalize your prospective dinner. On small waters or guts, I like to use a small rig of my best decoys. This is because there they are more noticeable, and should be, to near and distant ducks. In this case, a rig of 6 to 12 will do. It is a good idea to have a confidence decoy or two near to reassure your quarry. They can range from geese to swans or even gulls to relay trust. On small narrow ditches with nearby trees, crows, egrets in the water or even blue heron decoys will work. As with any type of still hunting keep everything as natural as possible. I have had some success with the new wind sock type decoys (if not overdone).

Carl Addison—Ring-necked Duck

Full size

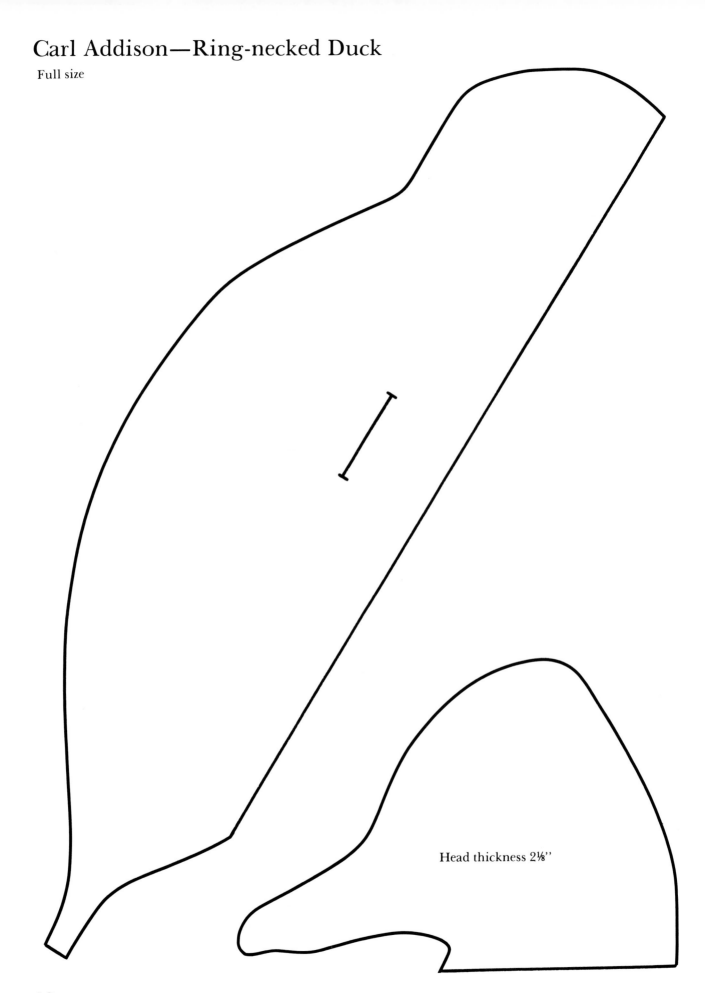

Head thickness 2⅛''

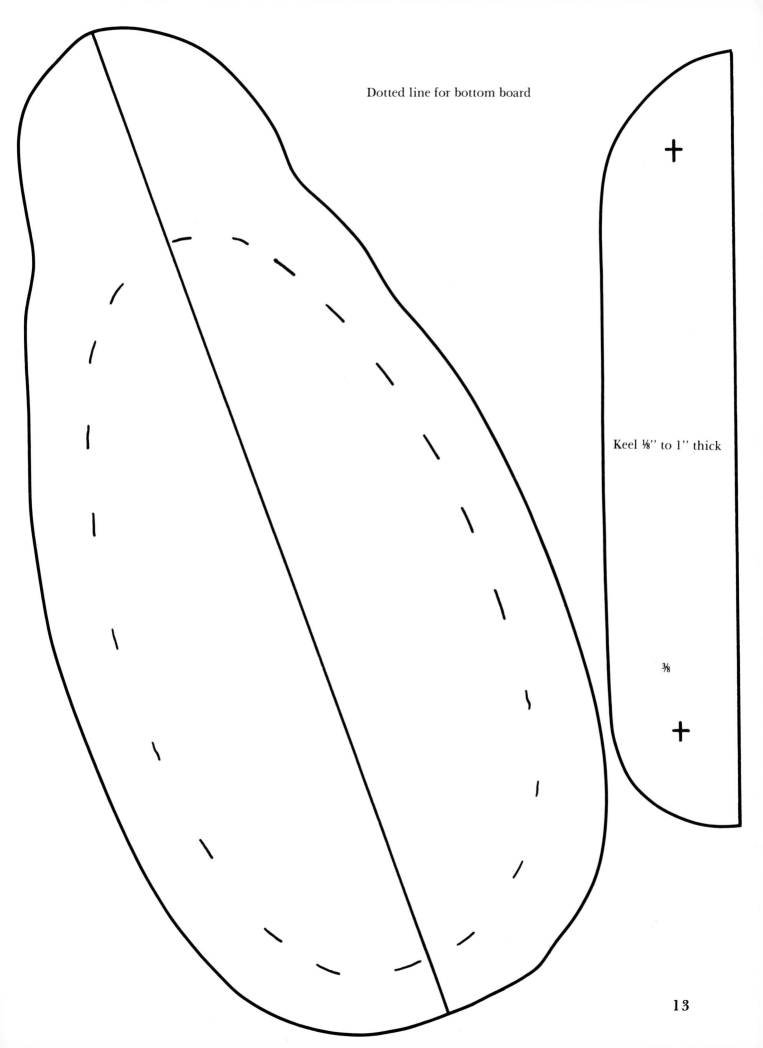

Dotted line for bottom board

Keel ⅛″ to 1″ thick

⅜

13

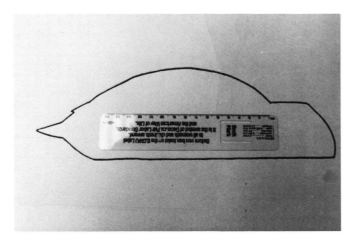

Profile body pattern.

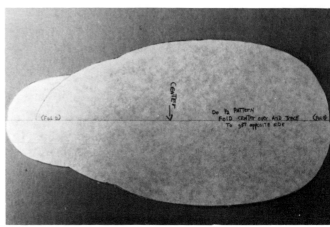

Plan view of body pattern.

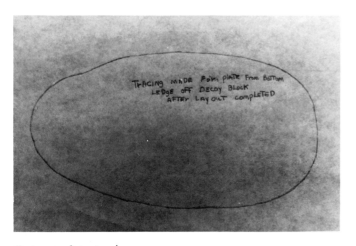

Bottom plate tracing.

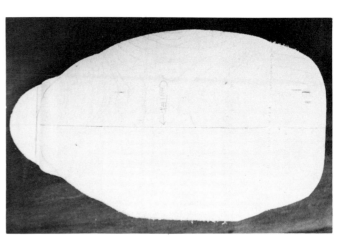

Bottom of roughed out block.

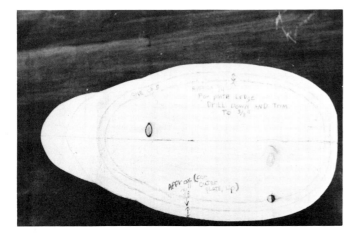

Bottom of block with layout for bottom plate.

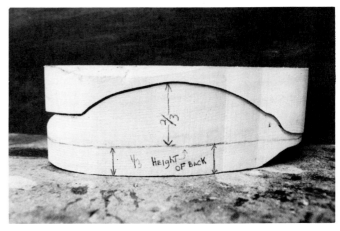

Profile of block band-sawed with excess cradle block.

14

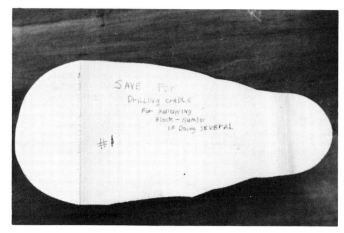

Cradle block used to square carved block for drilling.

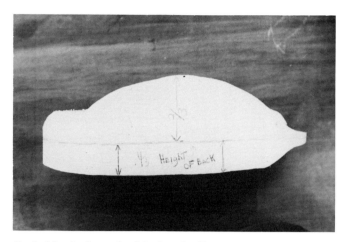

Body block shaped with drawknife.

Body block shaped with drawknife.

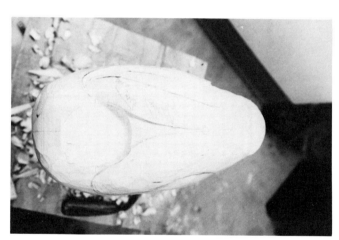

Center indentation carved.

Shaped block with side pockets drawn in.

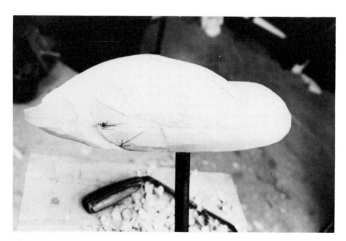

Contour directions.

15

Rounded body block.

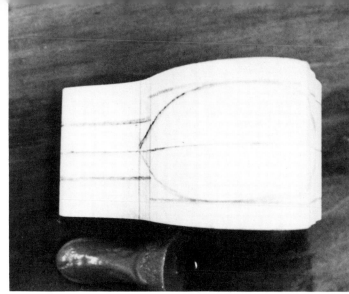

Band-sawed head with top view layout.

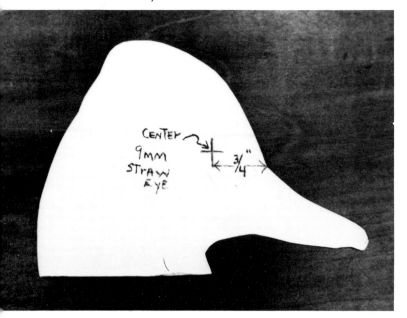

Eye location.

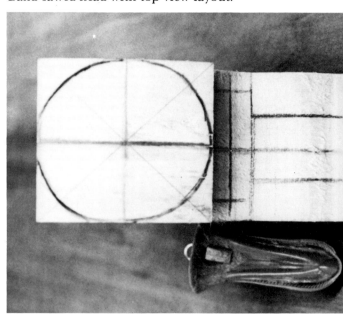

Band-sawed head with bottom view layout.

Bill delineation and cheek highpoint.

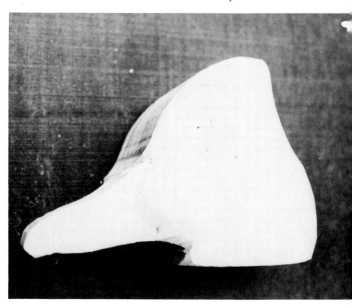

Shaping back of head to cheek.

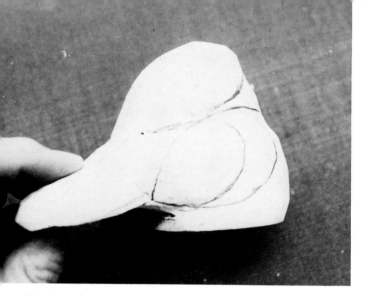

Cheek and crown contours.

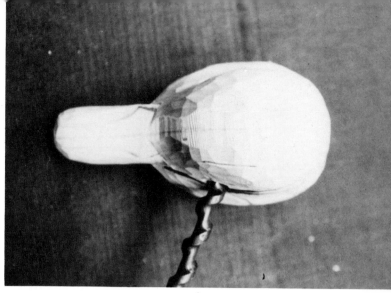

Drilling eye holes.

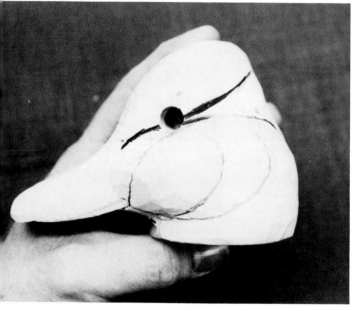

Cheek and crown flow lines.

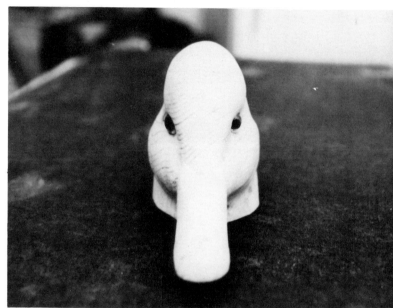

Sanded head with eyes set.

Drilling body with forstner bit. (note cradle).

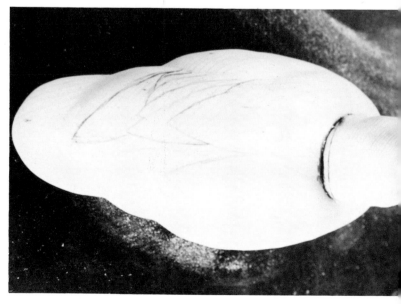

Finished carving with feather layout.

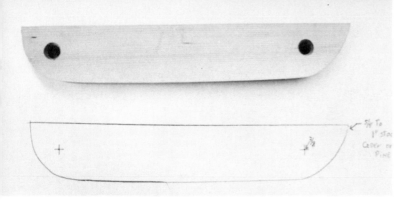

Profile of keel.

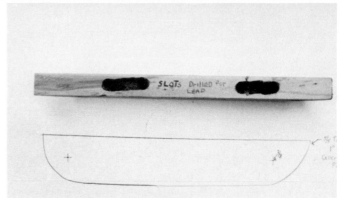

Top view of keel with holes drilled for lead.

Bottom board glued and sealed.

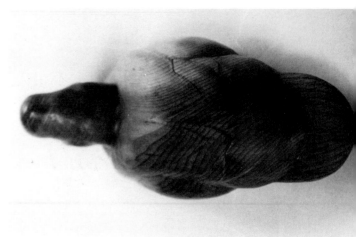

Top view of carved feathers.

Finished decoy sealed and ready for painting.

Decoy coated with gesso and pushed with brush to create "feathers".

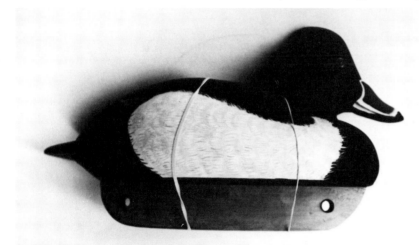

Keel held in place with rubber bands while floating for balance.

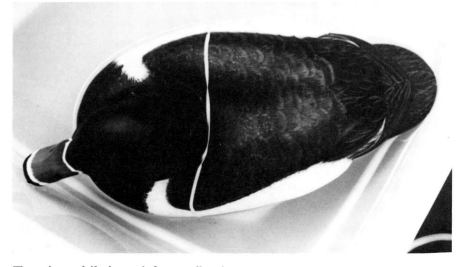

Top view while in tank for test floating.

Painting instructions for all projects begin on
page 208 and follow alphabetically by maker.

Robert Biddle

Baldpate

Bob Biddle was born in North East, Maryland in 1937 and grew up at Port Herman along the Elk River at the head of the Chesapeake Bay. He began hunting and carving hunting decoys at the age of 14, using wood found along the river.

In the 1960's Bob became interested in decorative carving and participated in most of the national carving shows, taking many First Place awards. Bob continues to make hunting decoys, all by hand, which he uses in North Carolina, Maryland, Delaware and New Jersey.

Bob feels that a hunting decoy should represent the personality of the duck it attempts to lure. He feels that the attitude of a decoy is more important than exact coloration, eye placement more important than eye size, and silhouette on the water more important than size of the block. Generally speaking he favors darker colors on his decoys rarely ever using pure white.

Bob collects antique decoys and feels that the great attraction to those old blocks today lies in their artistic beauty and simplicity of design. He contends that the old makers "knew their ducks" and in the interest of efficiency, stripped away the non-essentials and produced a completely functional piece; one that had everything it needed to draw ducks and no more.

Bob rates Ira Hudson as number one on the list of old master decoy makers and feels that Ira's decoys have all of the qualities that a decoy should have plus a certain personality that must have been a part of the maker himself.

Robert Biddle—Baldpate

Full size

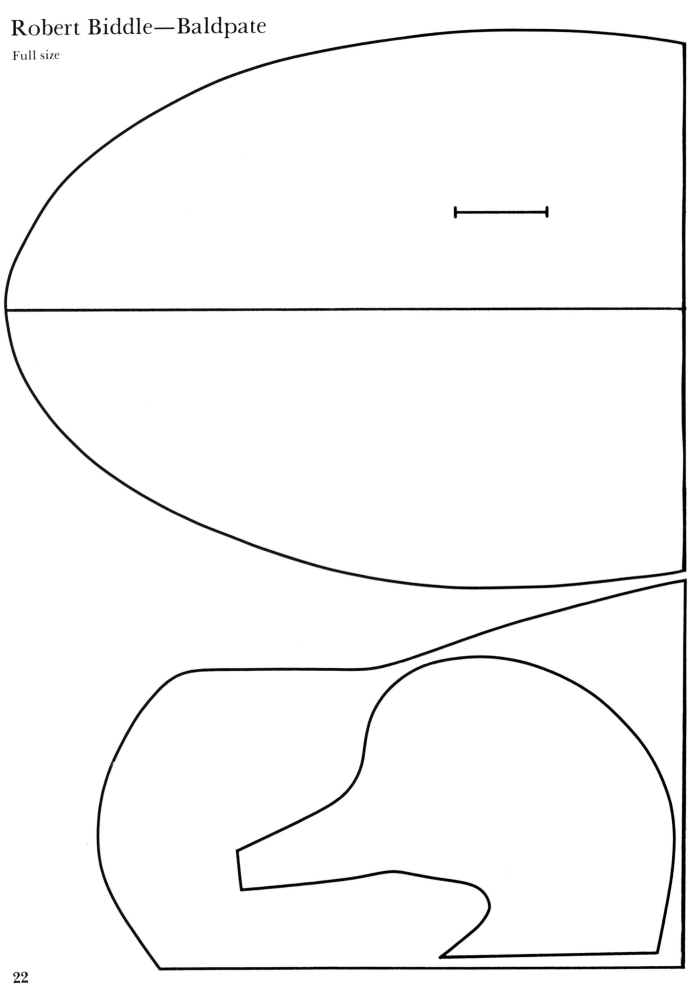

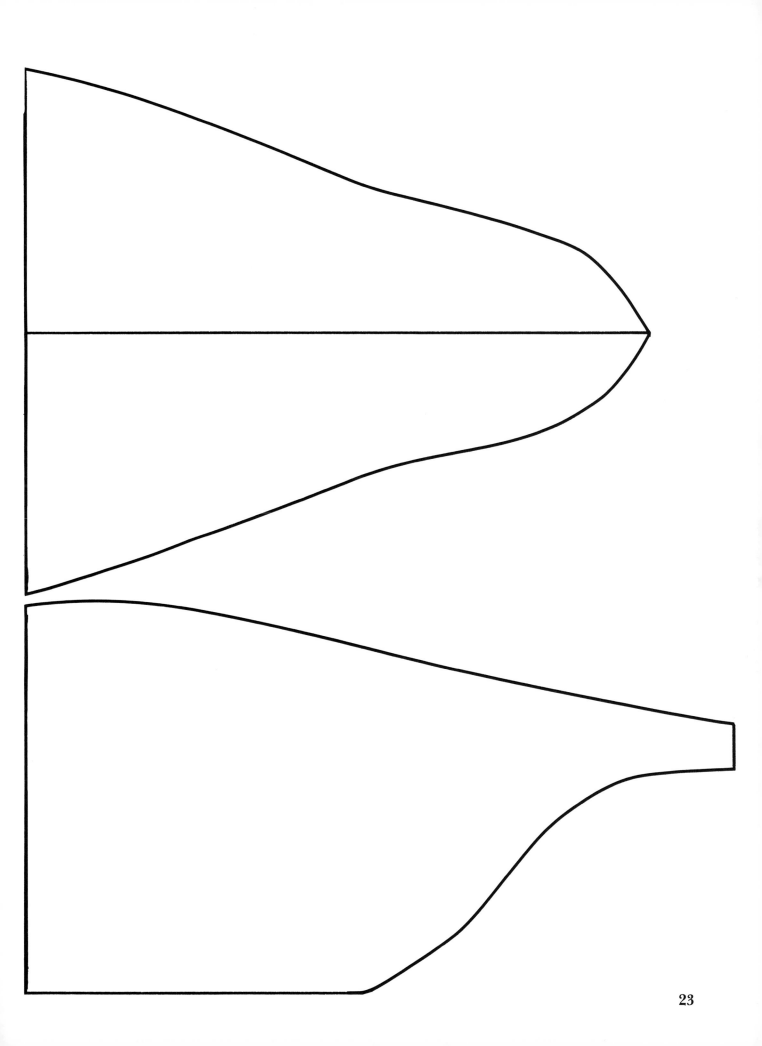

23

These are the basic tools of the trade: the hatchet, the drawknife, and the spokeshave.

Boldpate
by Bob Biddle

1 INCH SQUARES

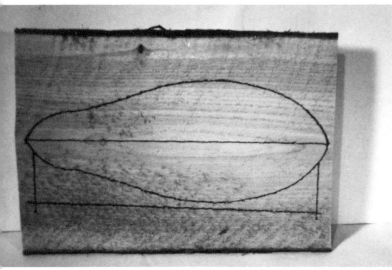

Patterns: I draw all of my own patterns. First, I put them on paper and when I have used them a few times and determined that they're just right, I transfer them to wood. For the body, I use half-patterns and turn them over for exact symmetry on both sides.

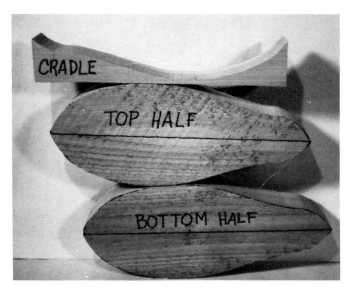

CRADLE
TOP HALF
BOTTOM HALF

In starting the body I mark the pattern on two pieces of 2" New Jersey white cedar plank—top half and bottom half. On one of the halves, I draw a cradle on the scrap portion of the plank to be used later for holding the body while bandsawing the profile. *Note:* The wood grain is straight along the center axis of the decoy. The cradle can be used for 10 or 12 birds before it becomes too chewed up.

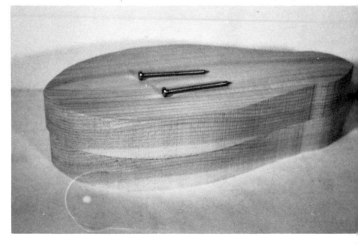

Top half and bottom half are planed down to a thickness of 3¾".

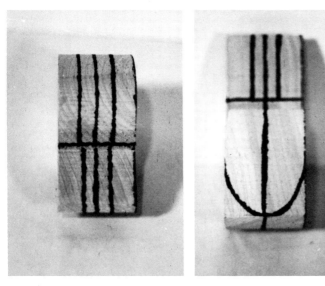

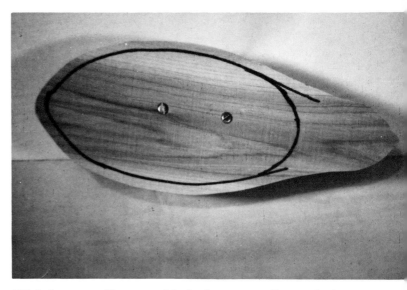

Head: A center line is marked around the entire head. Then I mark the bill width (⅝—11/16) inches on the baldpate) both top and bottom. I draw what I call, safety lines on the crown of the head, usually about ⅛" wider on each side than the bill. On the bottom I draw a semi-circle describing the shape of the back of the head at the base.

With the top and bottom of the body temporarily attached with pan head wood screws, I scribe a ⅜" safety line on the bottom of the decoy inside of which I will not cut when working the sides into the bottom.

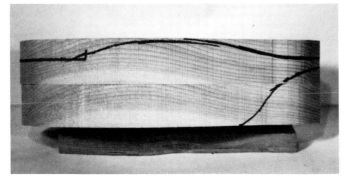

Turning the body on its side, I lay out the profile by eye, setting the base for the head about ⅞" below the high point on the back. This varies depending on whether its a high head or a low head decoy. This one is about medium height. *Note:* The vertical slash, which shows how far back the head will set on the body. This is one of the reasons the head should always be completed before starting the body. The setback is determined by visualizing the completed decoy and finished slope of the breast. A wide setback gives a more gradual breast slope—an "at rest" bird. Little or no setback portrays a bird swimming or one with a more alert posture.

The back is sloped towards the tail to achieve either a hightail or average tail profile. The profile under the tail is drawn to make it intersect with the safety line drawn on the bottom.

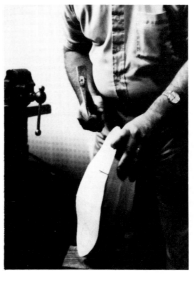

With my hatchet I rough out the top of the decoy. I start with a chop about 2/3 the way back to the tail, cutting towards the front of the decoy (marked in black on the side for purposes of illustration). This is slightly "up grain" and permits the first blow to remove a sizeable slab towards the rounding of the back. I continue on downwards to the breast taking care not to cut inside the line showing where the head will set on the body.

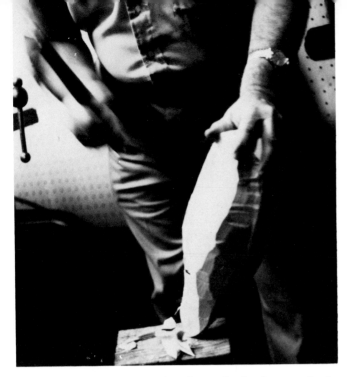

Turning the body around, I shape the back towards the tail; first one side and then the other. The blows on the tail end must be softer than those on the breast end to avoid splitting or denting the tail.

Notes on hatchet: I use an old lather's hatchet that is only moderately sharp. If it is draw knife sharp you cannot chop with firm blows and letting up on the strength of your chop, much like letting up on your golf swing, results in inaccuracy. My hatchet has a 2″ wide blade and a 11½″ straight handle. Many carvers are reluctant to use a hatchet for fear of destroying the block occasionally, but I feel that it is a great time saver and allows you a level of control in rough shaping the block that is unattainable in bandsaw shaping. If you use the same hatchet all the time it is amazing the accuracy you will develop in a very short time—usually after doing two or three birds. While chopping, you turn the body while looking down on it from about 30 degrees with respect to the center axis. This gives an almost infinite perspective that also is not attainable in bandsaw rough shaping.

Head: Using a Buck Bros. No. 3 straight ½″ gouge with only a slight curvature, I rest the bill of the head block against a 2″ cedar block which I have nailed to my work bench. The block measures 3½″ x 9″ and is nailed at the extreme rear of the block to avoid hitting the nails with the gouge as the block wears down. In front of the nails I bore ⅜″ holes and insert dowels for extra precaution against hitting the nails. I still change the block every time it gets worn about half way through.

With the gouge I form the eye channels first on the left side of the head. I work down the bill to the bill width safety line and cut a channel about ¼″ deep between cheek and the base of the head. Turning the head around, I make a series of cuts downward at about 45 degrees to round the back of the head.

After the left side of the head is roughed out, I turn the head over and do the right side. I begin the right side by holding onto the bill and cutting the eye channel from front to back. I also start rounding the back of the head to a point about half way down because it is easier at this spot and from that angle. In that same position I cut the groove between the cheek and base of the head. Turning the head I now cut down the bill to the width lines marked on both the top and bottom of the bill. This is the most difficult part because the other side of the bill is completed and the head doesn't set flat on the bench. I hold the head with the heel of my left hand while I'm cutting.

Safety Tip: Note that my hands and fingers are always positioned behind the cutting edge of the gouge. If the gouge slips it always goes into the block. (**NEVER CUT WITH ANY PART OF YOU IN FRONT OF THE GOUGE TIP.**)

Tip: I never set my gouge down. I have a wooden sheath for keeping my gouges and if a gouge is not in my hand, it's in the sheath. It only takes a soft touch against metal or sandpaper to render a gouge useless. I hand hone my gouge about once a month on a conical-shaped gouge stone, using 3-in-1 or cutting oil. I have used the same gouge for about fifteen years.

In about five minutes, after you get the hang it, you have your head roughed out. Note that I haven't cut inside any of my safety lines.

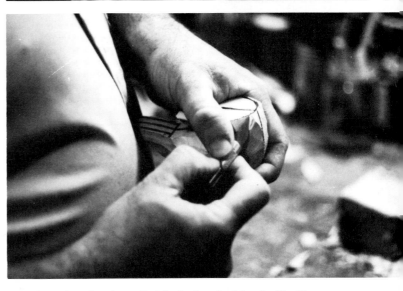

At this point I begin to finish the head with a knife. I have an array of knives that I use, but most often stick with a red handled Exacto with an "old" #24 blade or one of the outstanding knives made by Cheston Knotts of Wilmington, Delaware.

27

I sand only the bill and the very base of the head about half way around each side before mounting it on the body. It's easier to complete the head sanding with two hands after it's mounted. For the bill sanding I use 80 grit 1'' plumbers sand paper. I pull it between my left thumb and the bill. This method of sanding allows you to feel the flair of the bill through the sandpaper and thus shape the piece. I finish with the same types of strokes using 120 grit paper.

Body: To facilitate the further shaping of the body, I attach a tee-shaped steel bracket to the bottom with either two, or four, #12 1¼'' pan head wood screws to hold it in a regular machinist's vise that I have mounted on my work bench. I have the tee-shaped brackets welded at a machine shop out of 3/16'' steel. For ducks I use 2'' x 4'' plate and for geese and swans I use a larger plate made of ¼'' steel. For a large swan I use two brackets; one fore and one aft to balance the weight and avoid the great leverage created in working on a large piece in a vise.

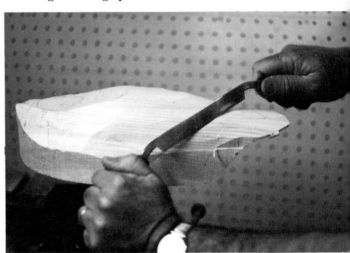

In my hunting decoys I bore a hole from the tip of the bill back into the head and drive in a #6 finishing nail for added strength in the bill. I make the hole slightly smaller than the #6 nail for a snug fit; set it about ⅛'' deep with a nail set; and fill it with Plastic Wood and sand it smooth after it hardens. Since I've been doing this, I've never had a bill break off in normal use.

I begin with a draw knife, which I keep razor sharp, working from the high point on the back of the decoy toward the tail. Turning the piece in the vise I drawknife the top, sides, and under the tail working down to the safety lines I drew earlier on the bottom. I take it out of the vise frequently to check for symmetry and to be sure the tail is parallel with the bottom and not flaired up or down on one side.

Next, I turn the bird around in the vise and work down the breast end with the drawknife, taking care not to cut through the line indicating where the head will set.

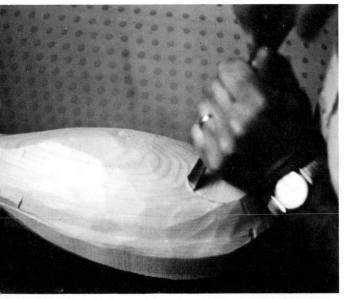

Using my same #3 Buck Bros. gouge I now cut straight down or slightly back cut the outline for the rear base of the head. This is why it's important to use a sharp pointed pencil to describe that line so you can get a good tight fit. With the gouge I clean out the necessary wood required to make the head set flat on the body. I keep trying the head while I'm cutting to get a good fit. If this is done carefully, the fit is so good that no filler is required. The head set in this way, is much stronger than it is if it's not set in.

At this point I go over the entire body with a spokeshave smoothing it to its near final shape.

Before separating the two halves of the body, I drill four pilot holes down through the top piece into the bottom piece. This is done for two reasons: 1) to insure I'll get the two pieces back together the same way they came apart, and 2) to keep the two pieces from rotating in the clamps during the gluing operation.

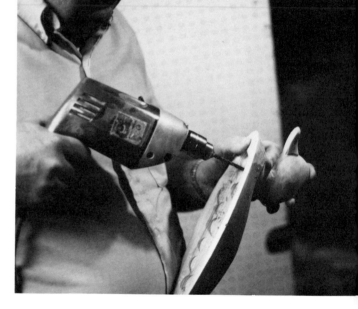

After drilling the pilot holes, I remove the plate bracket and separate the two halves. Using a drill press with a 1¼'' Multispur bit, I hollow the top and bottom halves and clean up the inside with a gouge if it needs it. I make sure there are no splinters sticking up to prevent a tight fit of the top half onto the bottom half. While the two pieces are separated I hold the head onto the top piece and drill a hole up through it and into the base of the head. I attach

the head with glue and a 3" pan head wood screw with a ¾" washer and tighten it down onto the body. If by chance the head doesn't fit the body properly, I put some wood filler under it istead of glue and tighten the head down on it. This forces the wood filler out around the crack and I smooth it out with acetone and a small, throw away glue or flux brush.

After the head is mounted to my satisfaction, I glue the two halves together with Resorcinol glue. I coat both surfaces and reassemble the two halves using nails in my four pilot holes to guarantee a precise fit. In spreading the Resorcinal glue, I keep it about ¼" away from the outside edge. The clamping will distribute the glue and if I put it too close to the outside edge it will only spill onto the outer surface of the decoy and have to be removed later.

With the four pilot nails in place I clamp the decoy with C-clamps using scraps of wood to avoid marring the surface of the decoy.

After at least 24 hours of curing time above 60 degrees Farenheit, I remove the clamps and again attach the tee-bracket to hold the decoy in the vise. I countersink the pilot nails and go over the decoy again with the spoke-shave, where necessary, to remove any glue spots or rough edges. I finish the forward base of the head blending it into the breast with a Sur form rasp and then sand the decoy all over. For this sanding I also use the 1" plumbers sand paper in much like a shoeshine motion. When the sanding is completed, I vacuum the dust off the decoy and remove the tee-bracket. After putting two grains of lead shot in the hollow decoy, I fill the bottom holes with filler and it's ready for painting.

Painting: I prime all knots and sap streaks with white shellac to keep them from bleeding through the paint later. I then prime the entire decoy with white (black or gray as appropriate) Rustoleum or with a color near that of the final coat as in the case of the drake baldpate breast. If a drake baldpate breast is primed in white and it gets scratched in use, it will stand out too vividly.

I paint all of my hunting decoys with oil paint. The paints I usually use are Rustoleum flat black and white, Ronan Superfine Colors which can be obtained from Becker Sign Paint Co. and artists' oils in tubes. To the artists oils I always add a little Rustoleum black and/or white to flatten and hasten drying time. If using tube oil paint I use mineral spirits for a medium, with a few drops of Japan dryer. With this mixture I can paint every night; i.e. it can be handled and painted once again in 24 hours.

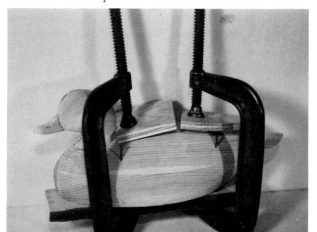

Dan Brown
Green-Winged Teal (Hen and drake)

Dan Brown was born in Dover, Delaware, in December, 1930. He grew up and went to school in Salisbury, on Maryland's Eastern Shore, and like many youngsters living along the vast Chesapeake Bay, developed a love of hunting, fishing and water sports.

For more than twenty five years Dan Brown has fashioned birds from wood in one form or another. First there were decoys for his own use, soon songbirds, shorebirds, hawks and owls were coming from his shop, as well as decorative waterfowl.

Realizing he had been collecting old working decoys found along the river for some time, many of which were crudely made, Dan began carving and painting more realistic and decorative birds for himself and for friends. A self-taught artist, Dan attributes much of the refinement of his skills to the advice of famous woodcarvers like Lem and Steve Ward of Crisfield, Maryland.

Dan Brown, today, is considered by many to be one of the finest wildlife woodcarvers in America. His creations are so accurate and lifelike one nearly expects them to swim or fly away...an advantage of working directly with wildlife in the field.

Over the years Dan has participated in all phases of competition, from working decoys, decorative decoys, lifesize decoratives to miniatures. He has been successful in each with numerous "Blue Ribbons" and "Best of Show Awards." Much of his competitive show time now is spent judging rather than competing.

Dan has exhibited in most major shows since the early 60's and his birds can be found in collections throughout this country and in a number of foreign countries. Today his work is mostly by commission, he is also represented by galleries both in the East and in California.

When not carving, much of Dan's time is spent on the Rewastico Creek, which borders his home, and in the nearby Salt Marshes observing and photographing bird and other wildlife. During the summer months his vegetable garden and trot line for Maryland blue crabs are high on his list of priorities.

Dan is the Curator at the Refuge Waterfowl Museum at Chincoteague, Virginia and was one of the Founding Fathers of the world famous Ward Brothers Waterfowl Foundation in Salisbury, Maryland. He currently resides near Hebron, Maryland with his wife Maggie. They have two married children.

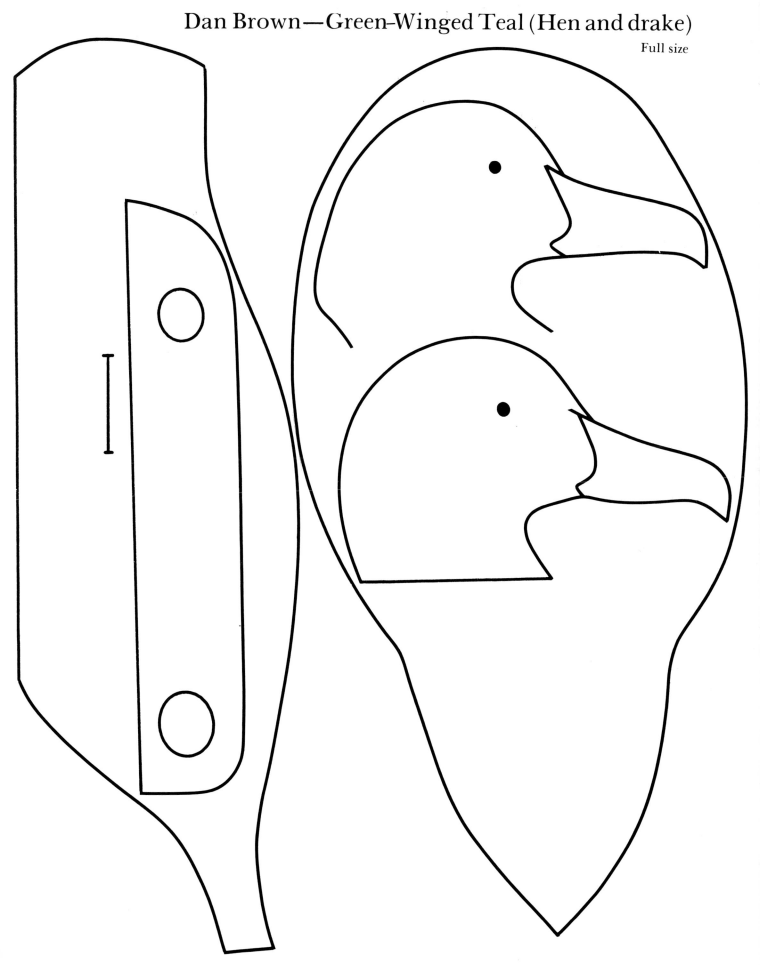

Placing profile pattern on block

Band-sawing plan view of body

Trimming excess off band-sawed block

Profile of head patterns traced onto block

Profile of head band-sawed

Center lining head

34

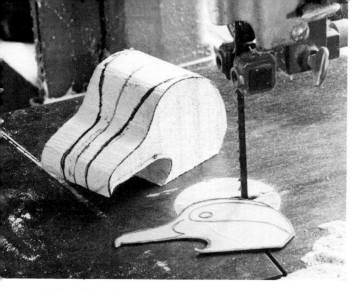

Head lined for trimming

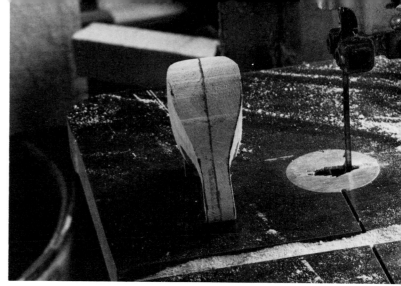

Head trimmed on band saw

Body trimmed with keel attached (note extra keel with holes drilled fore and aft for bottom weight line

Body block in vise

Body shaped with sur form rasp

Top view of body with wings cut in

Body hollowed with forstner bit

Front view of body

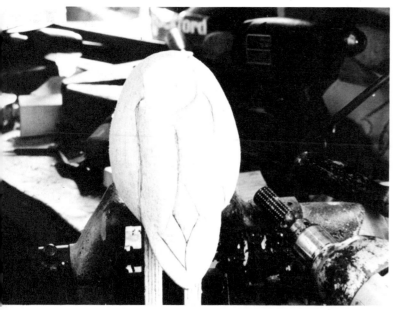

Top view of body with wing detail penciled in

Head in vise for shaping (note two pieces of wood to hold head without making dents

Profile of head in vise

Front view of head set onto body

36

Profile of drake decoy in vise

Profile of hen decoy in vise

Drake decoy with head detail

Hen decoy with "Bologna" wood body (This is polyurethane—dubbed "bologna wood" by Cigar Daisey—it makes a very good hunting decoy—note bottom board and tail insert.)

"Bolognawood" decoys in several stages

Finished hen teal decoy

Pair of teal decoys ready to paint

Profile of finished decorative Green-winged teal drake

Left view of finished decorative Green-winged teal drake

Right view of finished decorative Green-winged teal drake

Profile of finished decorative Green-winged teal drake

Delbert "Cigar" Daisey
Atlantic Brant

It is difficult to think of Chincoteague, Virginia without thinking of Delbert "Cigar" Daisey. Cigar was born in Chincoteague on March 6, 1928. He has always been associated with decoys and hunting, having been a guide, trapper and fisherman.

Cigar mostly makes gunning birds, however, he is well known as a decorative carver as well and is sought after by the best shows in the country to judge. During his competitive years he was a consistent winner.

"Cigar" has been the subject of many articles in national magazines. His carvings are in great demand by collectors everywhere.

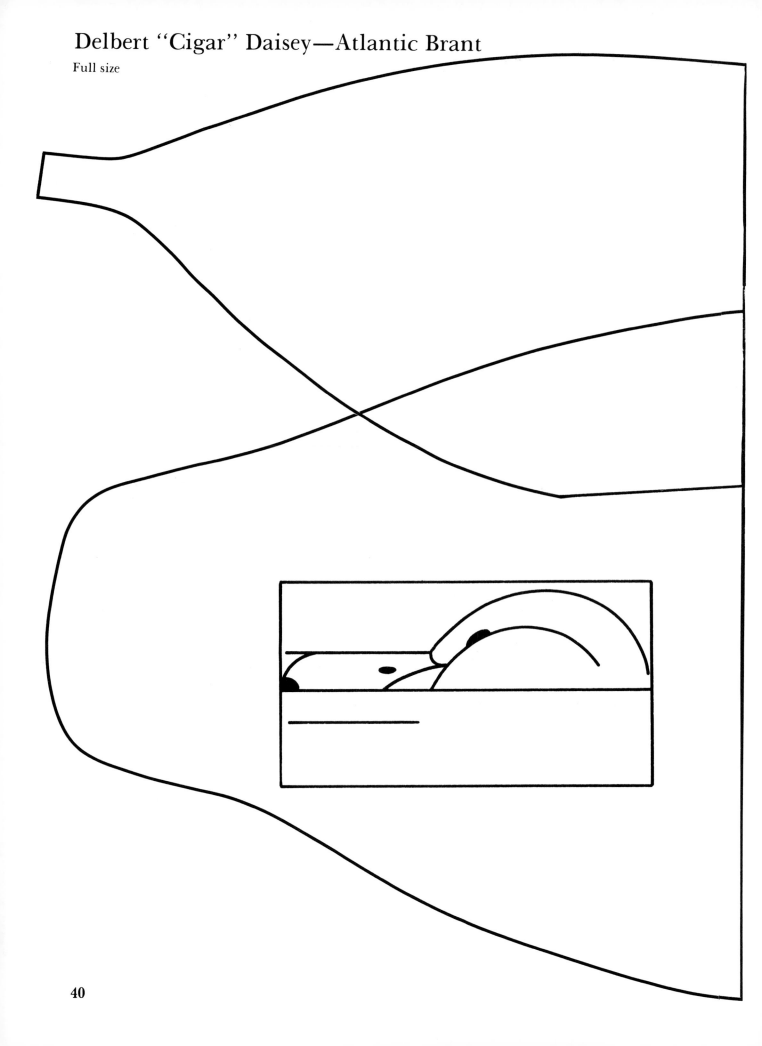

2¼''

Tacking profile pattern on rough block with push-pins.

Pattern tacked on cotton wood block. Note wood grain, this wood is widely used by Virginia carvers.

Bandsawing profile of body.

Bandsawing profile of body.

Bandsawing top or plan view of body.

Shaping block with use of hatchet to quickly remove excess wood, note center guide line

42

A profound statement, note guide lines on bottom of block.

Further hatchet work, note choking up on handle to almost shave with super sharpened hatchet (note-difference of opinion on sharpness of tools from carver to carver, it is an individual preference).

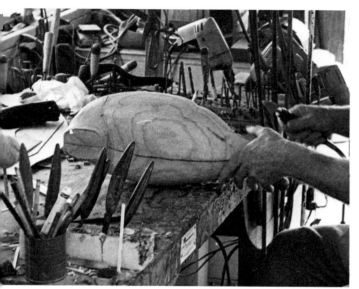

At work bench shaping with foredom tool using a Karbide Kutzall bit.

Checking for symmetry.

Shaping tail area.

Carving back of head with knife.

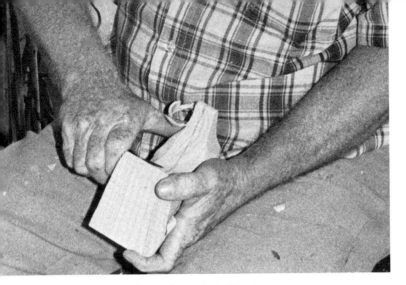

Carving under chin with knife.

Pencil guide lines and bill detail. Note—hands of the master.

Head placement.

Drilling eye holes.

Head placed again, note cork decoy in back ground, collection of Dan Brown. Mixing plastic resin glue.

Attaching head with glue and 6 2-1/2'' brads.

Shaping head to breast in a smooth flowing line using a knife.

Profile of decoy ready to paint

Head detail—note bill

Front view—note wide grain of cotton wood and the rough texture left by Kutzall bit. "Cigar" does not sand gunning birds—the texture helps keep colors flat

Rear view

Paul Dobrowski

Canvasback Hen

Paul C. Dobrowski, grew up and attended schools in the Rumson area of Monmouth County in New Jersey. He developed a love for the water having spent a good bit of his young life on the Shrewsbury and Navasink Rivers, as well as, the Raritan Bay and the Ocean. Paul became interested in Waterfowl Hunting at an early age and over the years has developed into a most proficient waterfowler.

His dissatisfaction with the equipment that was available, especially decoys, was instrumental in developing Paul's interest in decoy carving and the subsequent making of his own decoy rigs. In addition, to many decoy rigs which are applicable to specific species of birds to be decoyed, a wide variety of ancilliary equipment is required which includes: service boat (a garvy), layout boats, Barnegat sneakboxes, pond boxes, trailers, outboard motors, safety equipment as well as, guns and communication gear. All of this equipment which is specifically tailored to the task of operating under the most difficult weather conditions.

He is particularly adept at producing a rig of decoys capable of attracting ducks and geese to his layout. His ability to carve winning decoys is the result of his knowledge of waterfowl. The hours spent in the blind, in layout boats, in field studies, state sponsored bird banding projects and studying the habits and characteristics of the birds has enabled him to become one of the foremost gunning decoy carvers in the country. It becomes increasingly apparent that carving a good replica of the bird entails more than reading a "How to" book. It does require an intimate knowledge of the bird that can only be attained through the study of wild birds. Aviaries are interesting study pens, but all too frequently, disfigured (pinioned) birds, birds with feathers damaged by the confines of their home, or birds

hatched in captivity are a poor substitute for birds in the wild. While the bulk of Paul's experience lies with the live, wild bird, he has spent hours studying birds at a privately owned pond sanctuary which is stocked and maintained for a variety of diving and puddle ducks by local conservationists. In addition, Paul has worked with young waterfowlers in the New Jersey Waterfowl Association and the Ducks Unlimited Greenwing Programs and has held offices in both programs.

Paul has been carving for approximately 20 years and competing for 10 years. He has compiled a record of blue ribbon winners that includes the most prestigious shows in the United States and Canada. A catalog compilation of his most impressive wins is presented in the attached list.

While working on the decoy for this book, it made me realize just how many friends over the years have shared their opinions, ideas and techniques with me. They have been a constant source of encouragement in helping me to produce a fine working competitive hunting decoy.

Carl Becker, Fairhaven, NJ, was one of the first people to inspire me to start carving my own decoys. Weekend breakfasts in Carl's kitchen, brings forth a change of hats. I arrive to find him in a Chef's hat and when the coffee cups are empty, he donns his old carvers cap and we critique each other's most recent carving, and talk over ideas, experiences and upcoming shows.

Thanks to George Walker, Chesterfield, NJ, for his contributions to my knowledge of what makes a good carving.

Al McCormick, Westbury, L.I., for sharing his expertise and encouragement and producing a basic, simple working decoy.

Most importantly, I want to thank Ralph Walsh, Oceanport, NJ, for his continued inspiration, direction and help in completing the decoy carving presentation contained in this book. I have yet to meet another person that has such analytical dedication to producing as life-like a decoy carving as is possible.

His endless hours of research, his Aeronautical Engineering background and personality with regard to reference materials, photographs, carving aids, and painting mediums has given me a new (world approach) and awareness of this art form.

I often think that Ralph feels, if it flys, I can build a better one!

I am so glad our friendship goes beyond ready reference.

Last but not least, thanks to the many other carvers and waterfowl hunters for their shared memorable experiences and their continued friendship.

DATE	EVENT	PLACE
1977	1st Best of Show—Canvasback Drake	U.S. National (open Gunning Division) Melville, New York
1978	1st Best of Show—Black Duck	Great South Bay Waterfowlers Association
1979	1st Best of Show—Brant	
1980	1st Best of Show—Canvasback Hen	
1980	1st Best of Show—(open Decorative Head) Canvasback Hen	
1980	1st Best of Show—Atlantic Brant	Greater Snow Goose Decoy Contest, Chincoteague, Virginia
	2nd Best of Show—Green Winged Teal	
1980	2nd Best of Show—(Working Rig Division) (12) Black Duck Decoys	Set in Bayshore Area
1980	1st Best of Show—Atlantic Brant	World Championship Wildfowl Carving Competition—Ocean City, MD.
1981	1st Best of Show—Bufflehead Hen	(Lem and Steve Ward Shooting Stool Division)
1984	1st Best of Show—Canvasback Hen	Note: These winning decoys form a permanent exhibit at Ward
	3rd Best of Show—Mallard Drake	Wildlife Museum, Salisbury St. College, Salisbury, MD.
1978	1st Best of Show—Canvasback Hen (Amateur Decorative)	Canadian National Exhibition, Toronto, Canada
1979	1st Best Diving Duck—Broad Bill Drake	International Hunting Decoy Contest, Clayton, NY.
1980	1st Best Puddle Duck—Mallard Drake	
1981	1st Best Goose—Atlantic Brant	
1983	1st Best of Show—Buffle Head Hen	This decoy is permanently displayed at the 1000 Island Museum, Clayton, NY.
1983	1st Best Diving Duck—Canvasback Drake	Ohio Decoy Collectors and Carvers Association—Gunning Decoy Contest
	1st Best Diving Duck—(Decorative Head) Canvasback Drake	
1979	1st Best of Show—Mallard Drake	New Jersey Ducks Unlimited—Hunting Decoy Contest Award provided that the decoy was the subject placed on commemorative ashtrays at all state dinners in 1980.
1986	1st Best of Show—Canvasback Hen	Pacific Southwest Wildfowl Arts. California Open—Service Class/Gunning Decoy. This is the decoy shown in this book celebrating the creation of working decoys.

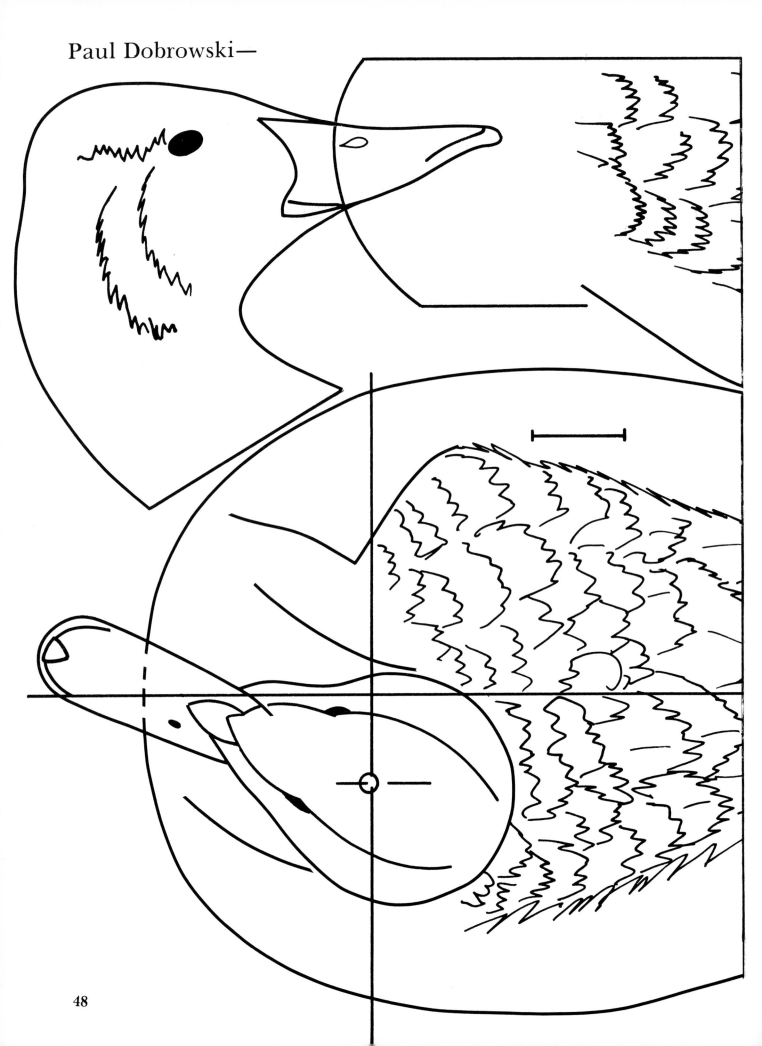

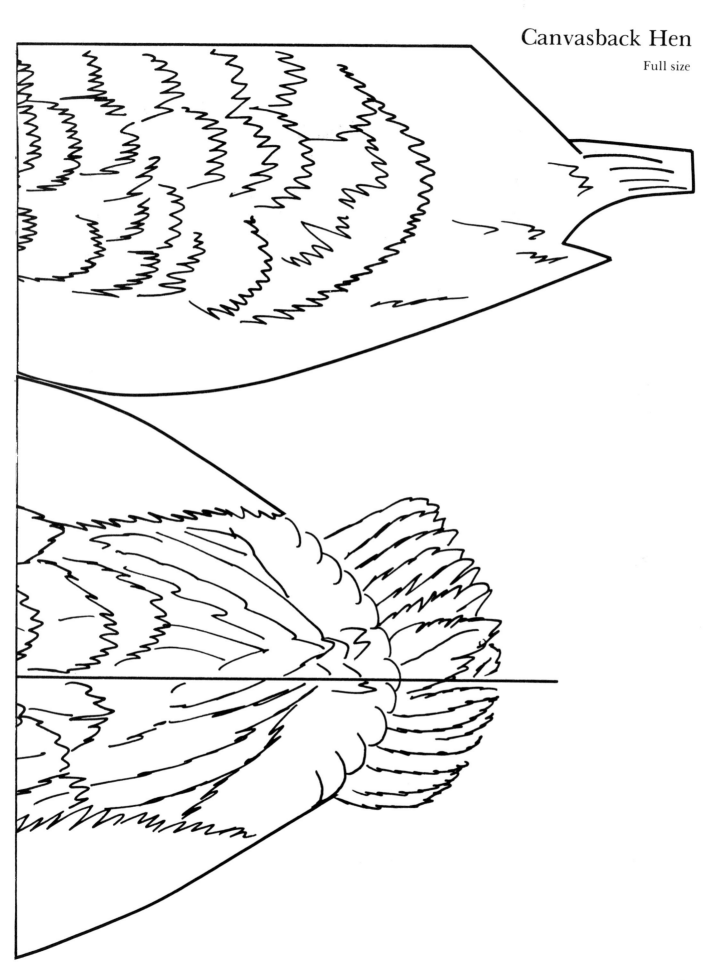

Reference photographs, photo (lower center) formed basis
for detail drawings and pattern.

Reference photographs.

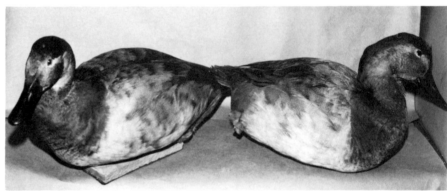

Reference mounts, (study material for color).

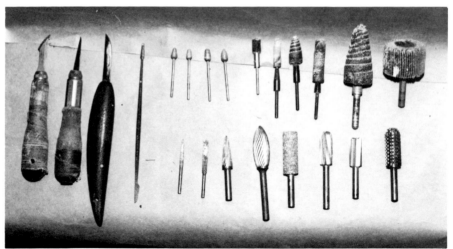

Typical tools—layout and burrs used.

Observe live bird for reference.

Reference material—banding canvasbacks. Specimen being observed prior to being released to it's natural habitat.

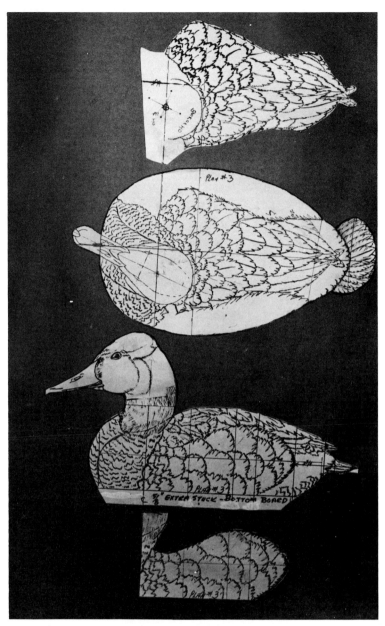

Basic drawings developed from photographs.

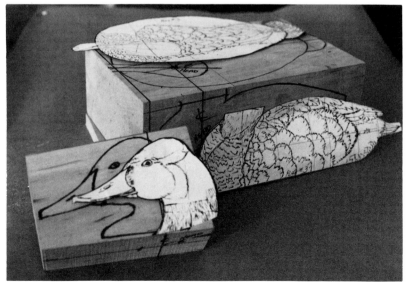

Block preparation and pattern layout.

51

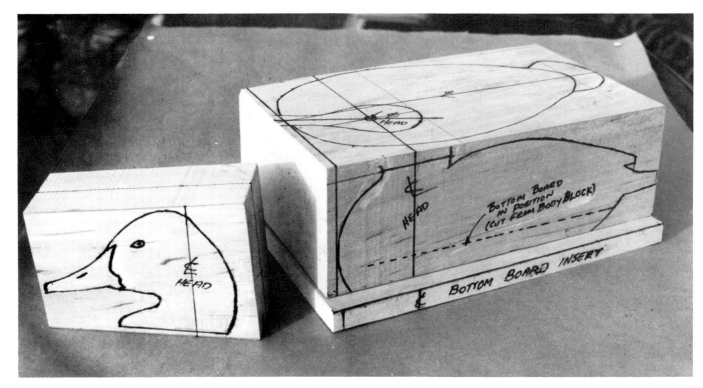

Patterns assigned to block. *Note:* Bottom board cut from same block to assure homogeneity of finished decoy.

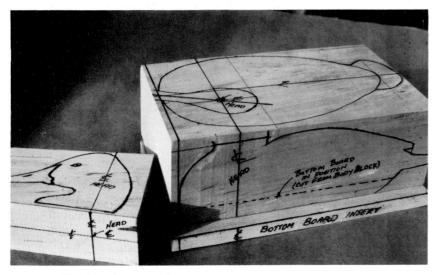

Block and pattern layout.

Sawing side pattern.

Sawing out top pattern.

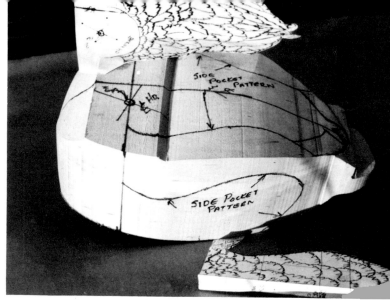

Side pocket pattern layout.

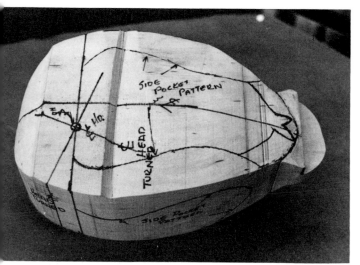

Mark-up side pocket and head location from top pattern.

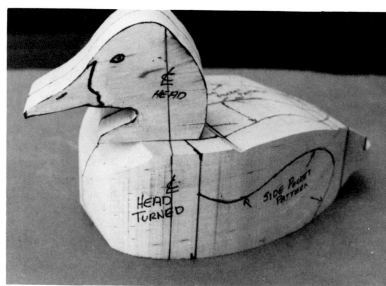

Block assembly—lay up.

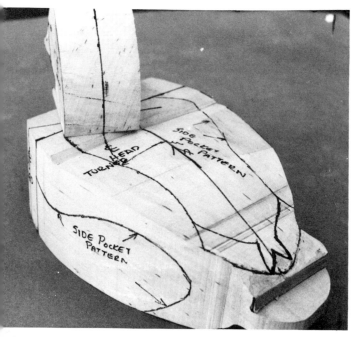

Rear view—block assembly.

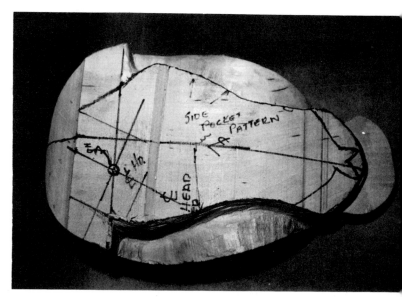

Side pocket pattern, cut-out establishes accurate side pocket.

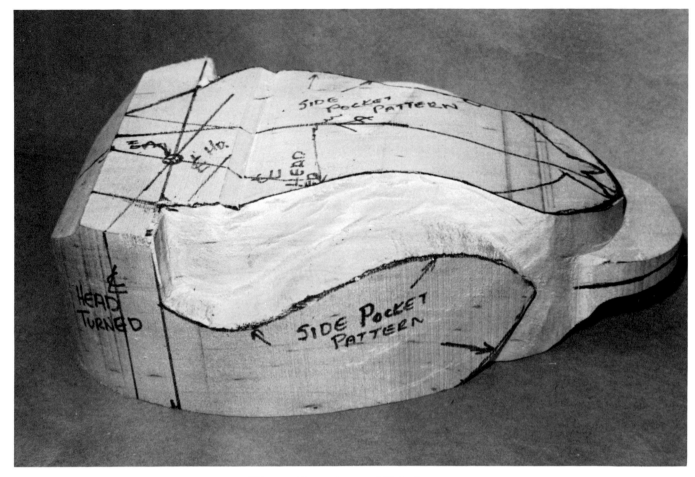

View—side pocket established.

Top and front view. Profile of side pocket cut in. Top front of chest rounded.

Front view.

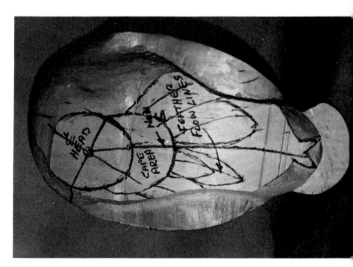

Top view.

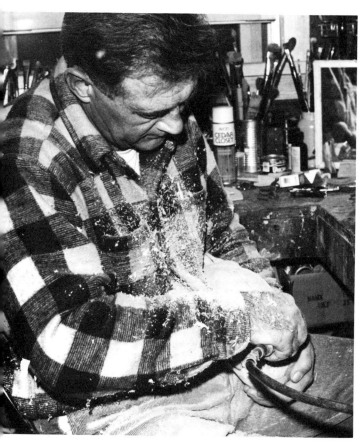

Round off—side pocket cut out.

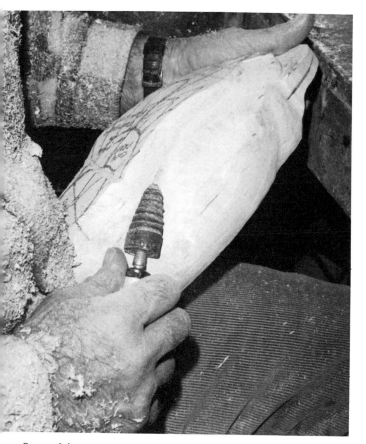

Smoothing out radius on side pocket.

Smoothing side pocket with cone shaped sanding tool.

Preliminary inspection.

Pencil layout develops flow-lines on decoy. *Note:* Side pocket and chest color lines defined.

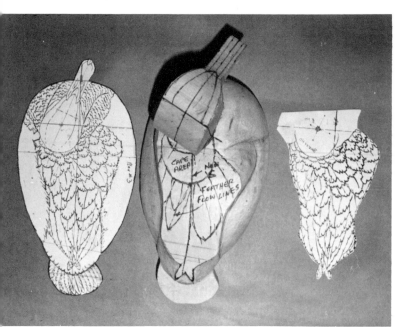

Pattern layout with shaped out block.

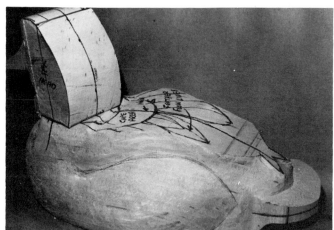

Positioning head/block relationship.

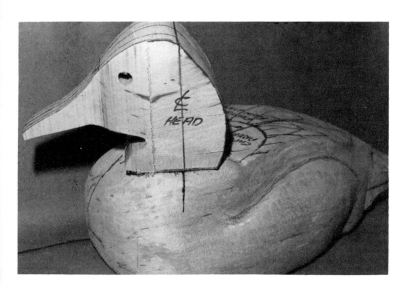

Side view head/block.

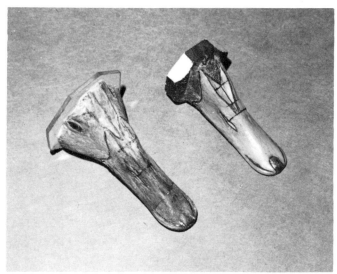

Study bills with layout lines.

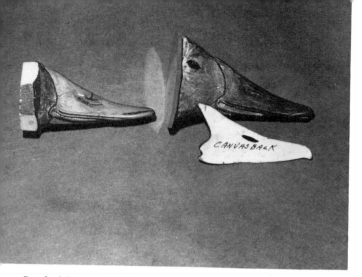

Study bills and bill layout pattern.

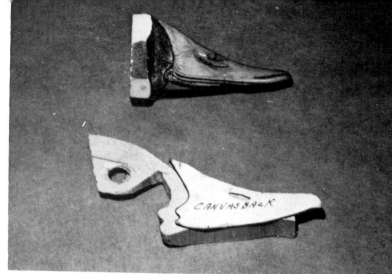

Study bill pattern. *Note:* "Saw out" from head establishes pattern for bill.

Head and pattern.

Saw out from head serves as pattern for bill detail.

Head and pattern.

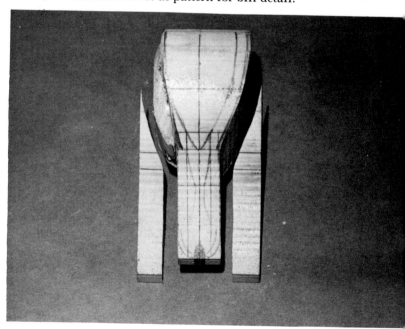

View of saw out.

57

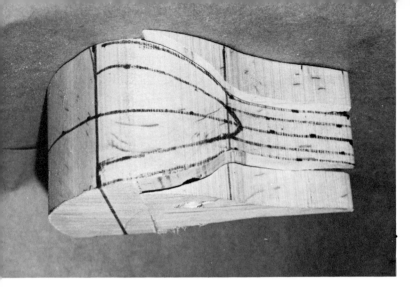

Top view—head saw out.

Front view—head saw out.

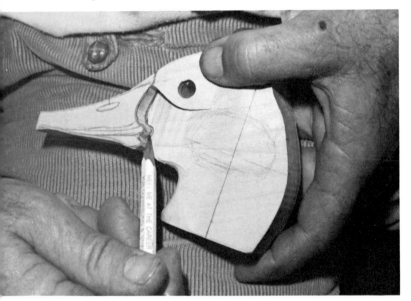

Head with bill layout pattern.

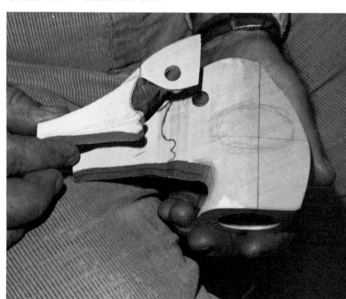

Bill layout pattern.

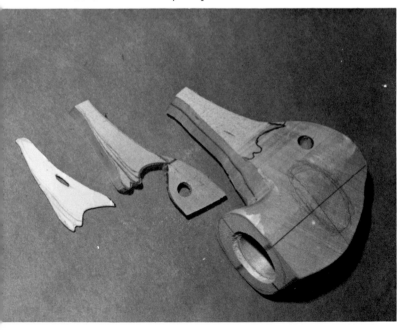

Bill pattern sequence.

"Saw out" bill pattern.

58

Hollowing head. (To improve decoy bouyancy and establish self-righting capability.)

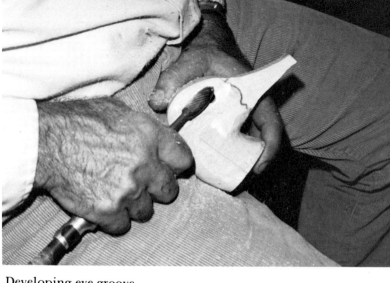

Developing eye groove.

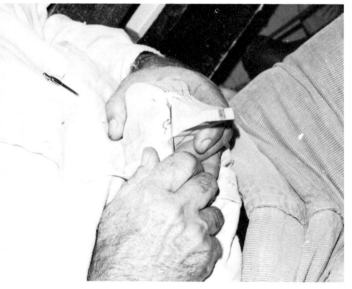

Establishing bill/head intersect contour with knife.

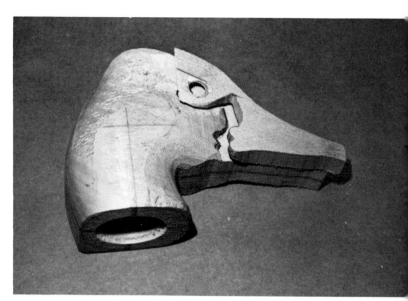

"Saw out" pattern establishes bill contour.

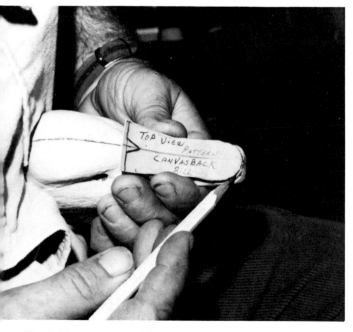

Top bill pattern establishes plan/view of bill.

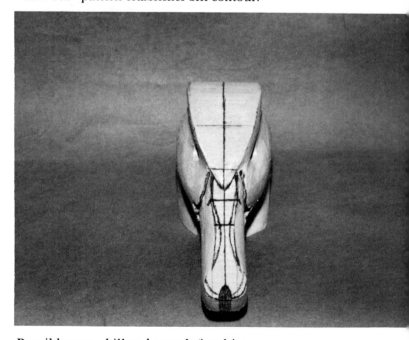

Pencil layout—bill and eye relationships.

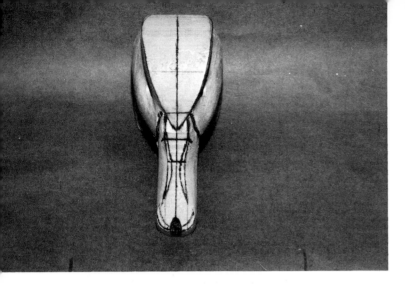

Pencil layout bill/head relationships.

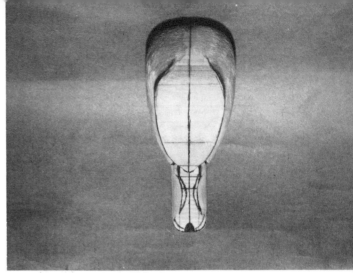

Top view—pencil layout head/bill contours.

Rear view—head/bill mark up.

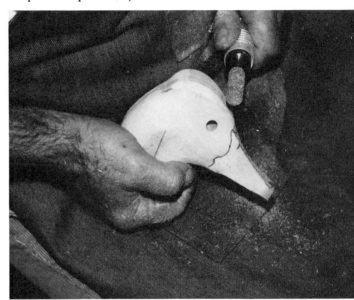

Round out bill/head contours. *Note:* Approximately 40 degree angle down from top of head centerline.

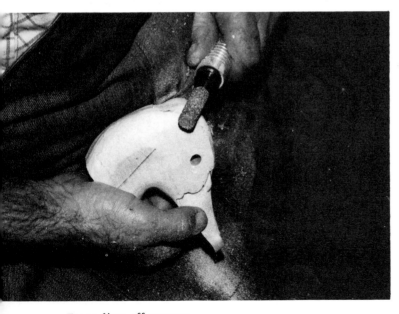

Rounding off corners.

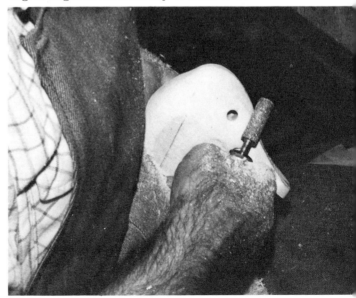

Rounding off corners. Bevel from top of head   40 degree angle toward cheek.

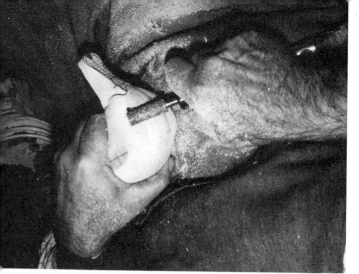

Rounding off corners.

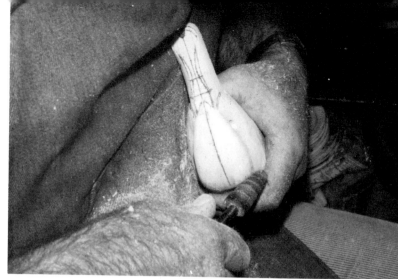

Conical sander smooths contour.

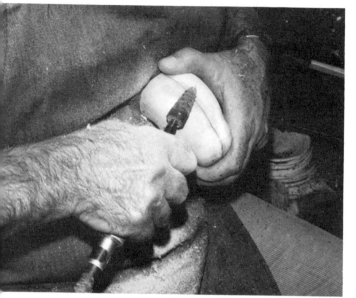

Smoothing contours with conical sander.

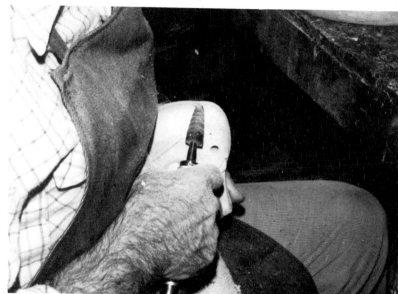

Contouring with conical sander.

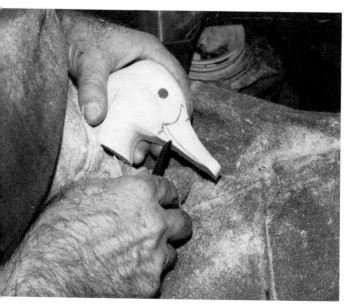

Lower mandible cut.

Lower mandible cut, note sliver.

61

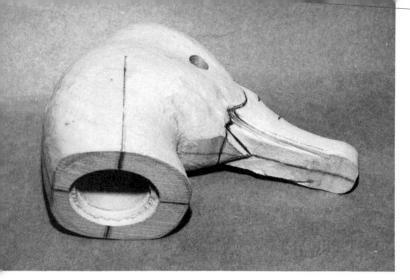

Lower mandible roughed out (critical to bill character).

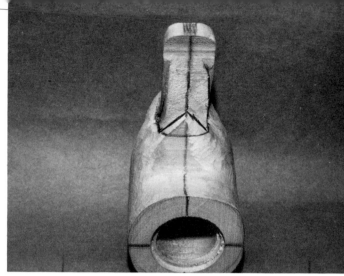

Underside view lower mandible.

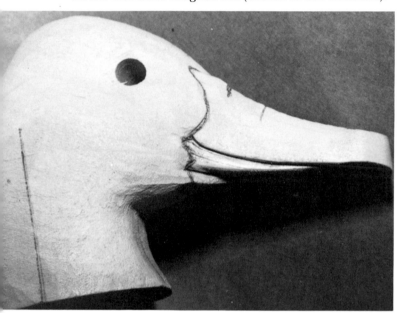

Bill detail.

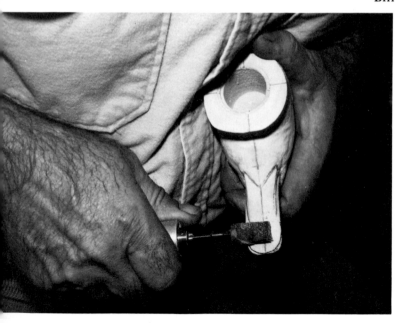

Lower mandible relief (curve cut at bill tip).

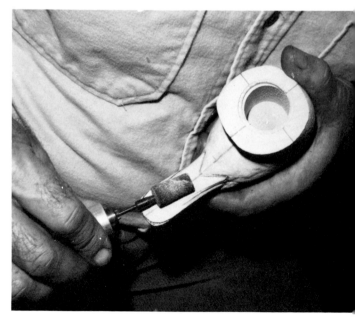

Lower mandible, longitudinal depression.

62

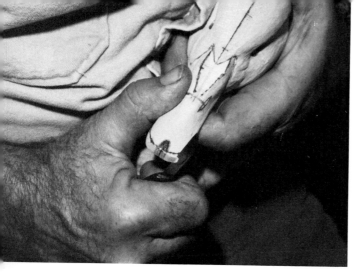

Bill tip contoured with a knife.

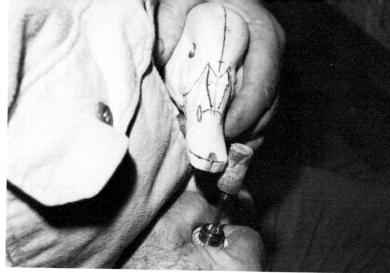

Sanding bill tip.

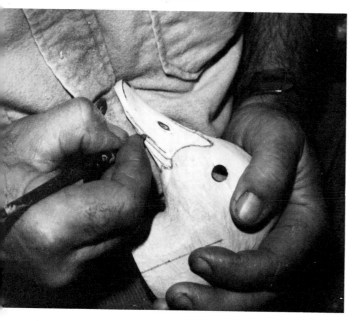

Awl used to create grooves on upper mandible.

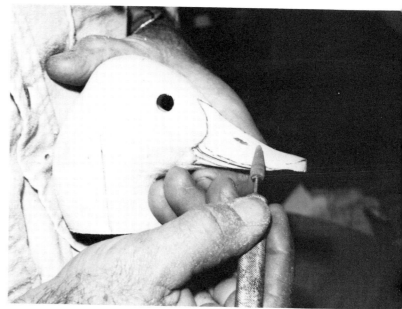

Cone shaped abrasive rubber cratex used to polish nostril area.

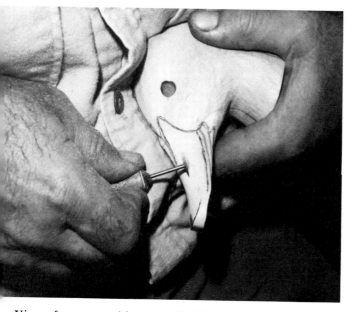

View of cutter working nostril with saw blade type cutter.

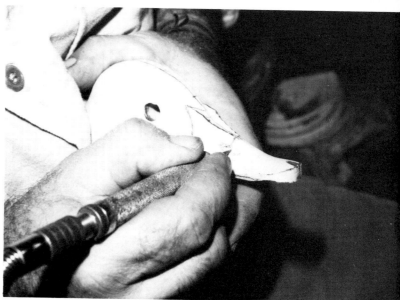

Nostril opening shaped with small cylindrical cutter.

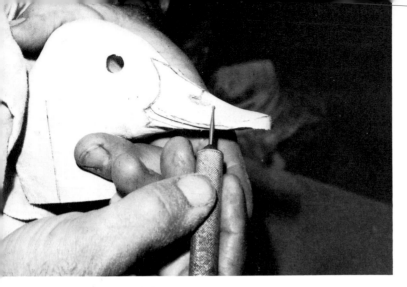

Lower nostril groove.

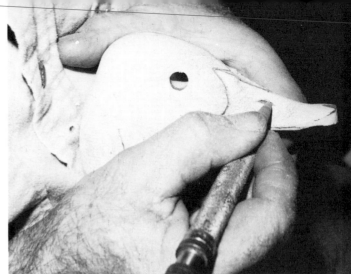

Shaping inside nostril.

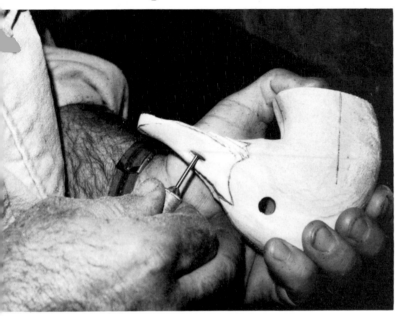

Saw type cutter used to rough out nostril.

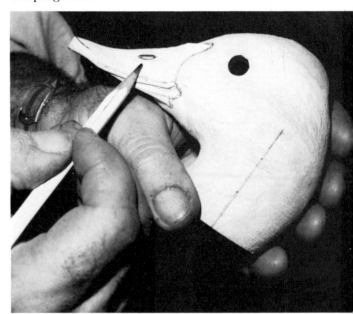

Pencil mark-up highlights nostril area.

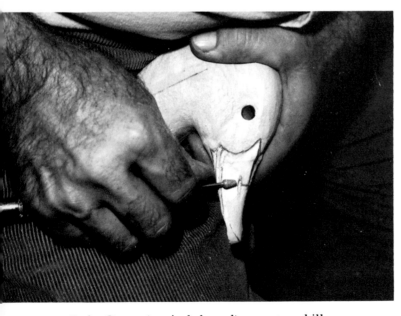

Ruby Carver (conical shaped) to contour bill.

Ruby carver used to develop concaved contours of bill.

64

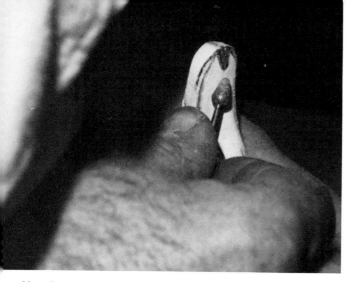

Shaping bill contours with ruby carver.

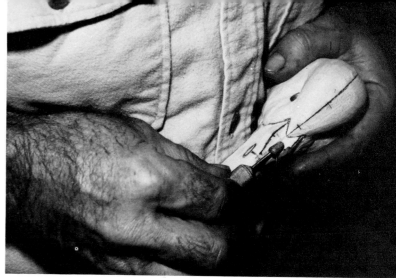

Shaping upper—bill cavities with ruby carver.

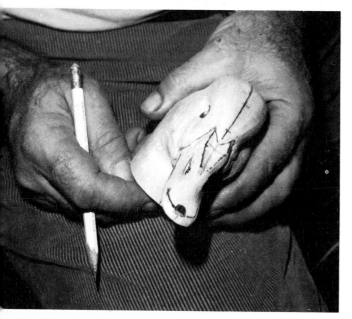

Pencil layout enhances critical areas of bill.

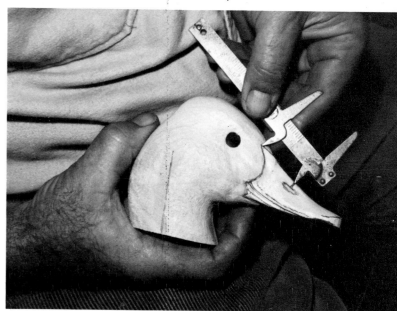

Establishing nostril location. Caliper data taken from study bill.

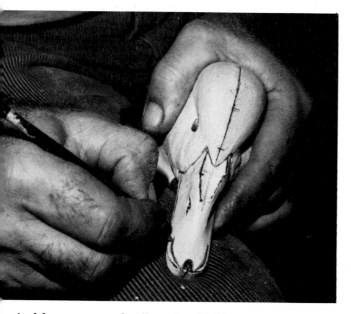

Awl forms groove detail on tip of bill.

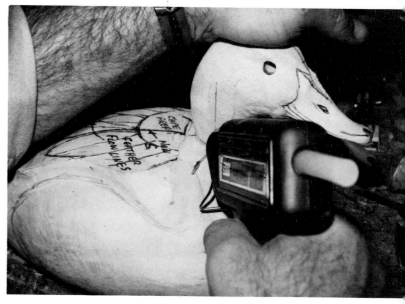

Hot glue to temporarily fasten head to body.

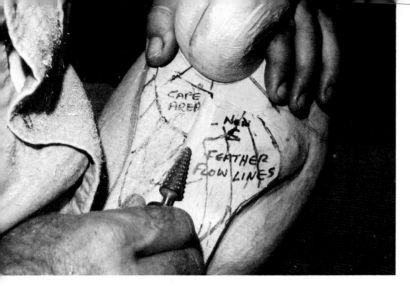
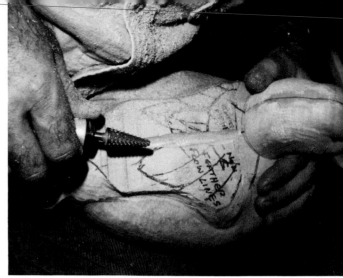

Head in place, conical bit forms groove on back between feather tracts.

Groove detail in back area.

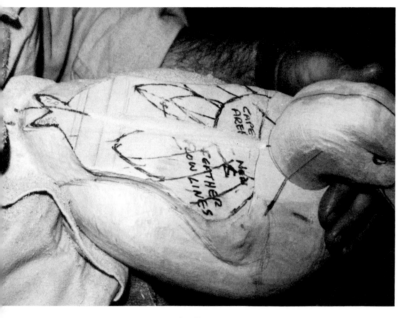
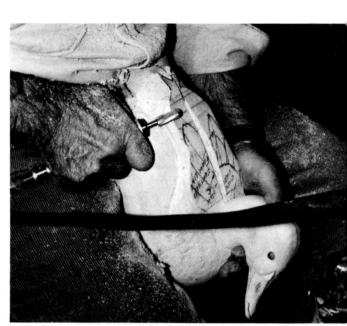

Rough out groove in back.

Rough out scapular areas.

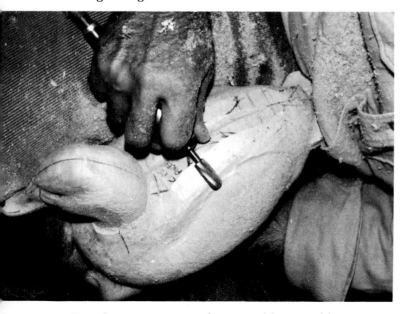
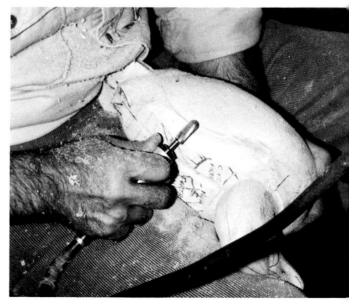

Rough out upper scapular area with router bit.

Rough out with router bit.

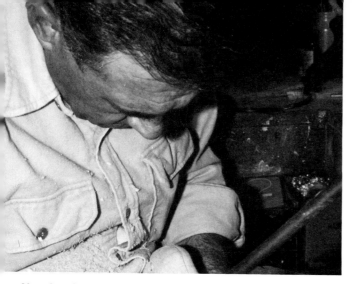

Shaping forward wing area.

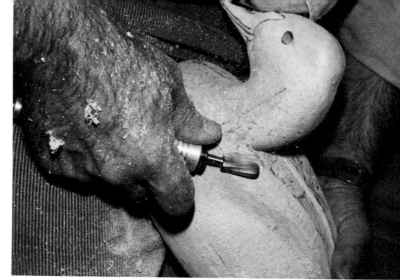

Shaping cape area.

Contouring breast into head.

Another view of breast/head area.

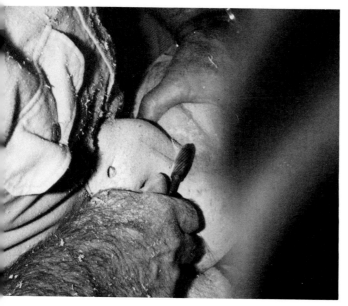

Contouring head/body.

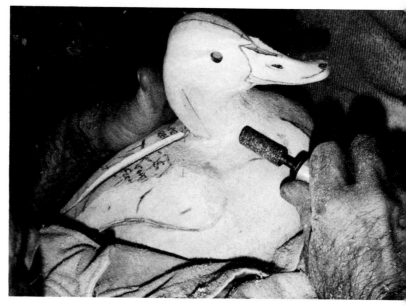

Smoothing out contour.

67

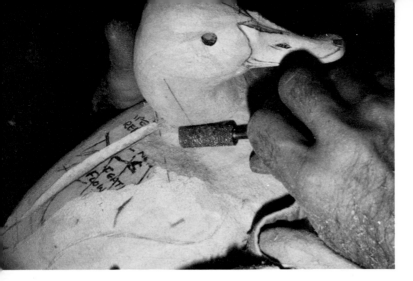

Smoothing out head/breast area.

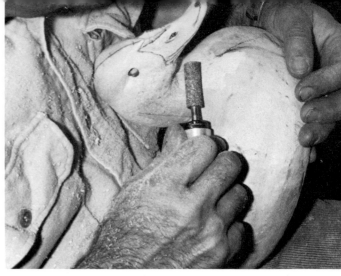

Shaping transition areas, head/breast.

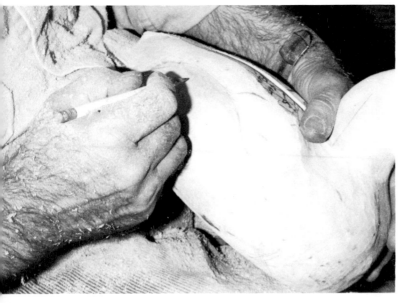

Light pencil lines applied to assist in establishing continuity in flow lines.

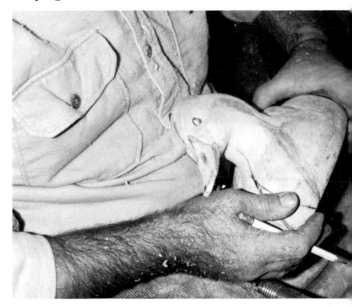

Lines help develop breast contours.

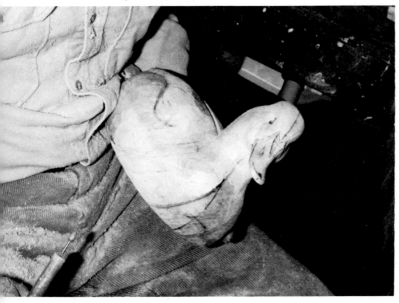

Lines assist in developing continuity in head/breast contour.

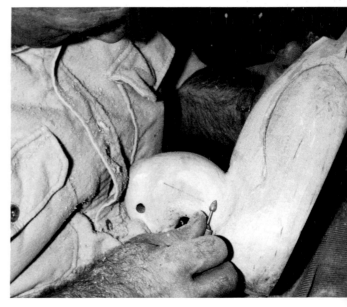

Ruby carver used to work out head/chest area.

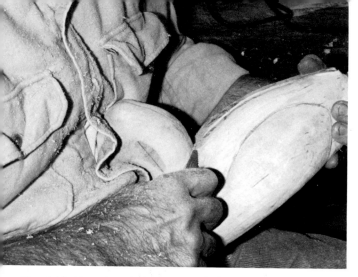

Head/body area. Shape around back of head area.

Ruby carver used to shape front of head and chest area.

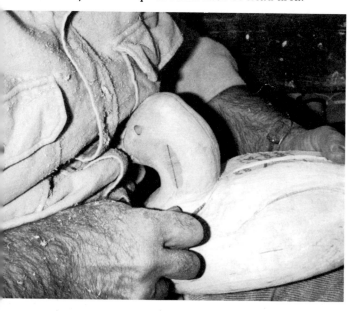

With a small tapered burr, shape back of head where it meets body.

Knock out hot glue secured head. (Use of dowel to knock off tacked head)

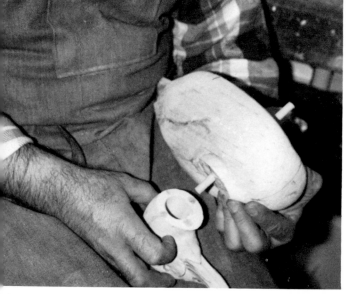

Separated head from body where it was secured for preliminary shaping.

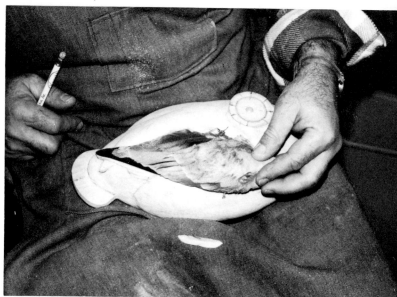

Primary feather location established with assistance from an actual wing.

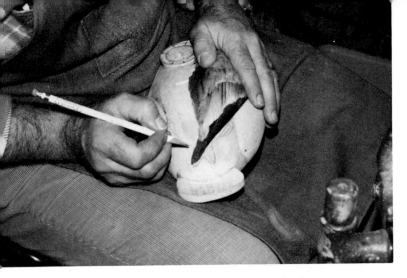

Primary is checked by use of an actual wing.

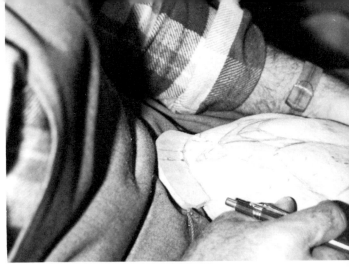

Pencil layout feather groupings.

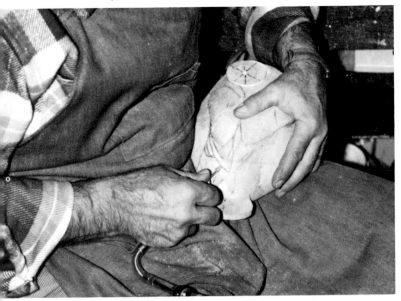

Relieving primary/tertial groups.

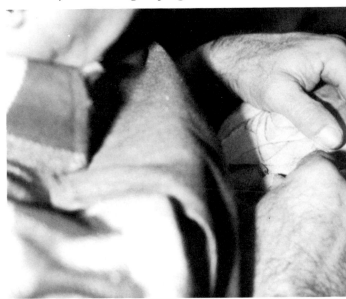

Working on feather groups.

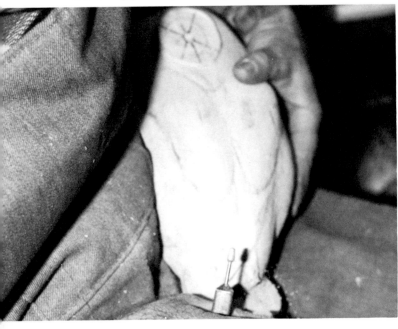

Primaries relief carved.

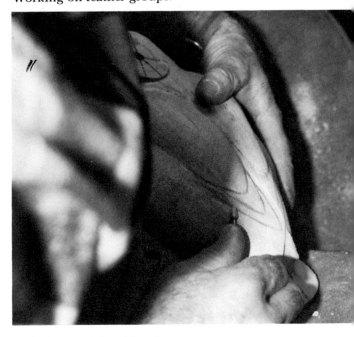

Defining tertials with ruby carver.

Marking out bottom board (bottom board cut from bottom portion of 5'' body block to ensure homogenity of grain and prevent shrinkage problems).

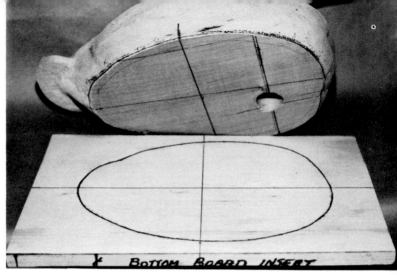

Bottom board insert traced from body.

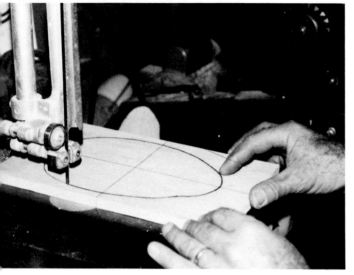

Cutting out bottom board. First cut overall outside diameter.

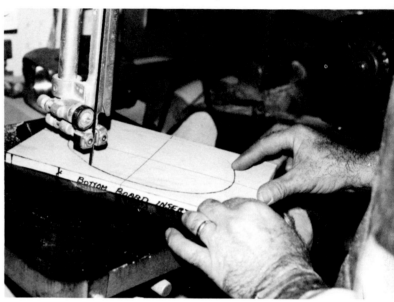

Cutting out bottom board.

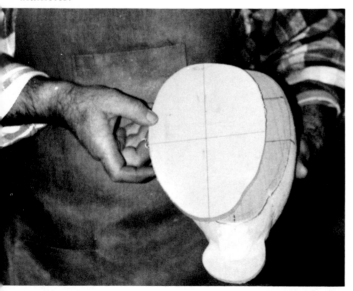

Cardboard pattern made of bottom board insert to serve as future reference pattern and as layout for drilled lightening holes.

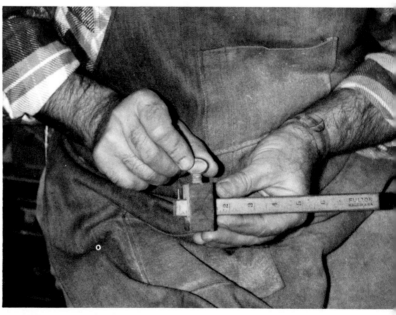

Marking gauge serves to establish bottom board contour to suit wall thickness at insert (⅜'' from outside edge).

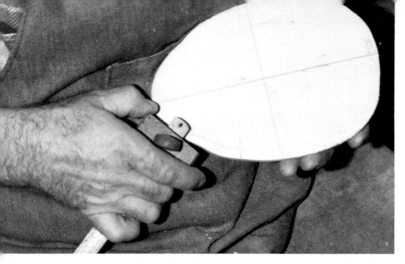

Scribing bottom board pattern to establish board insert wall thickness ⅜".

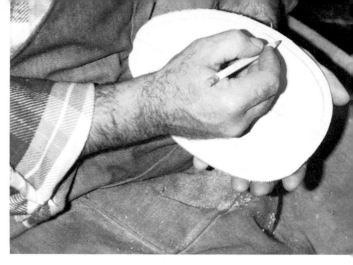

Pencil mark up on pattern to emphasize scribed line (⅜" in from outside edge).

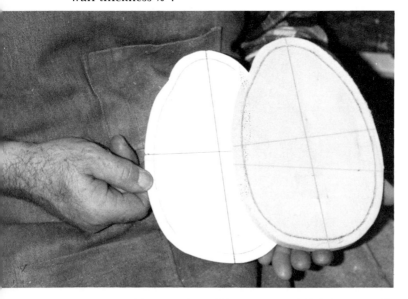

Pattern and bottom board insert to establish insert wall thickness.

Removal of ⅜" of material from bottom board to fit decoy hollow-out.

Bottom board pattern transferred to decoy.

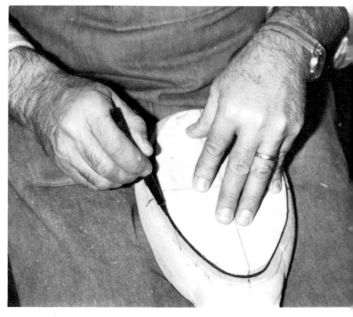

Pencil layout of bottom board insert. *Note:* ⅜" in from outside wall edge.

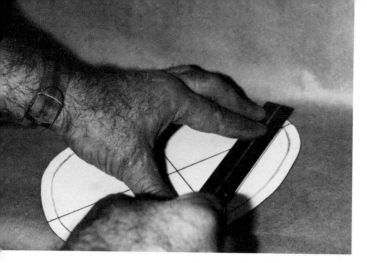

Bottom pattern serves as layout for lightening drill holes.

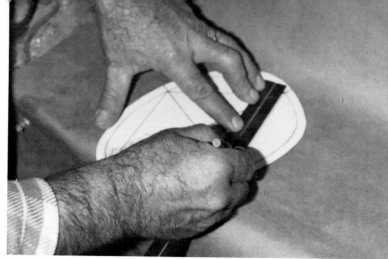

Layout (preliminary) lightening hole pattern.

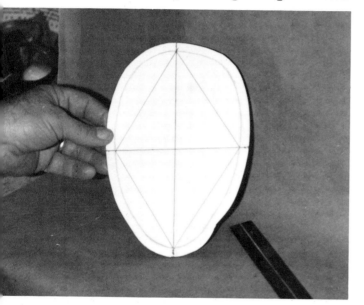

Prime layout for lightening hole layout to ensure and retain a structural wooden web within the hollowed decoy.

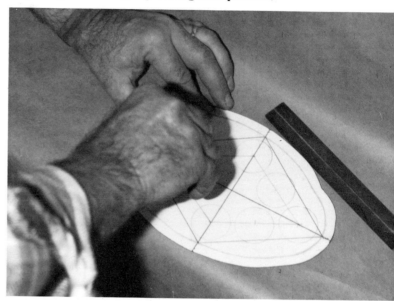

See next.

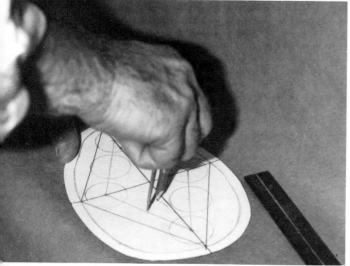

Compass layout of prime lightening holes tract. (Lightening holes planned to retain a structural web of wood to improve strength of decoy and to reduce "seasoning problems"). (Honeycomb design)

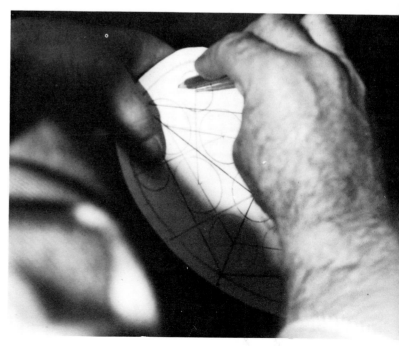

Compass—layout secondary (smaller) lightening holes.

73

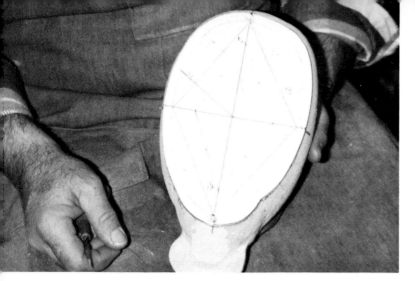

Lightening hole layout on bottom pattern.

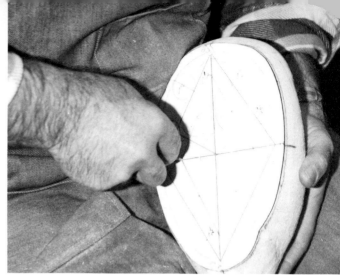

Transfer lightening hole locations to decoy body. Awl used to strike centers.

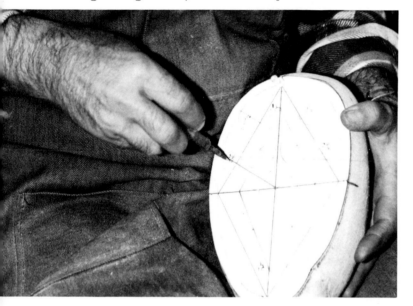

Awl in action.

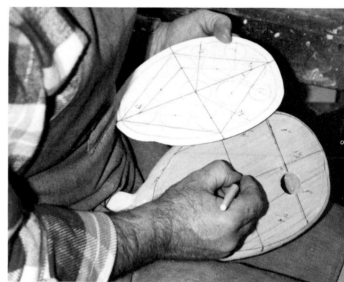

Penciling in center hole locations.

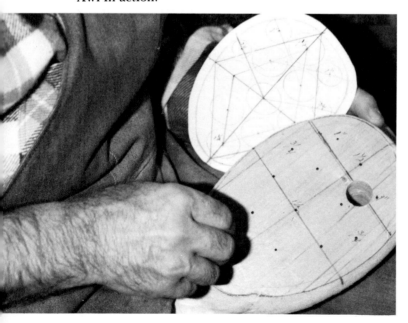

Lightening holes penciled in to assist in locating bores in body.

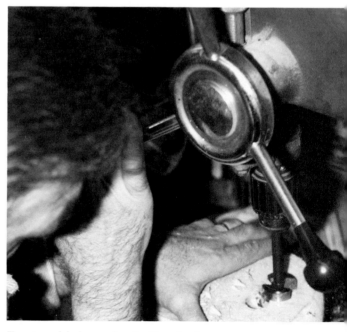

Forstner bit is used to hollow body.

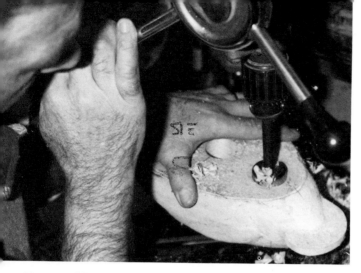

Forstner bit in drill press hollowing decoy body.

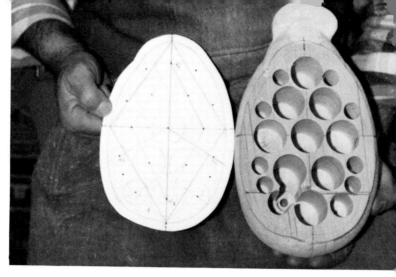

Hollowed decoy bottom and hole location pattern.

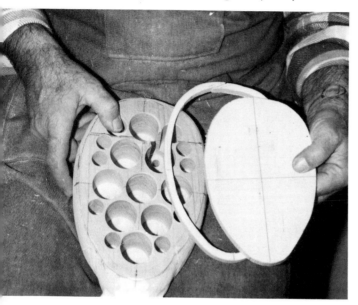

Hollowed decoy body—bottom board saw-out and scrap from bottom board to ensure proper side wall integrity.

Forstner bit used to remove "structural" web to enable placement of inserted bottom board. (Recess in bottom to receive ½" thick bottom board).

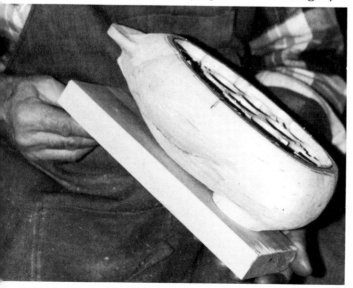

Holding fixture is used to establish support of decoy body for accurately "milling" or routing out insert cavity (½" deep to receive bottom board).

Holding fixture must be leveled (note wedges) to maintain ½" deep cut.

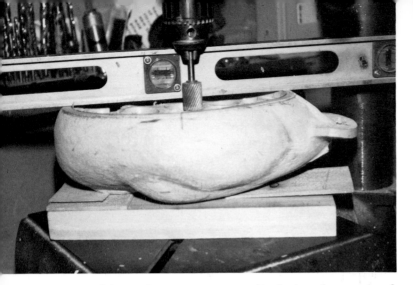

Level is used to ensure perpendicularity of cutter head with decoy body.

Routing out peripheral for insert board. *(Note:* Drill press spindle with milling cutter in place is brought into contact with bottom of decoy then advanced ½" and the drill press spindle is locked.

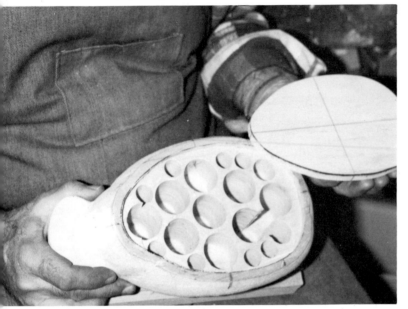

Body prepared for installation of insert board.

Hollowing head with forstner bit. (Head is hollowed to improve decoy buoyancy and self righting capability and also improve head attachment durability).

Hole saw used to cut a plywood washer from ¼" thick plywood. (Washers used to attach head to body and "T"/nut-caps on inside of bottom board).

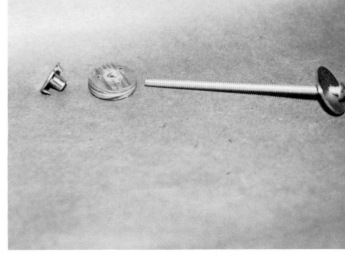

Tee nut plywood washer and head retention screw shown in assembly sequence.

Five minute epoxy is mixed in preparation for cementing tee nut head retention assembly in place.

Tee nut is pressed into plywood washer.

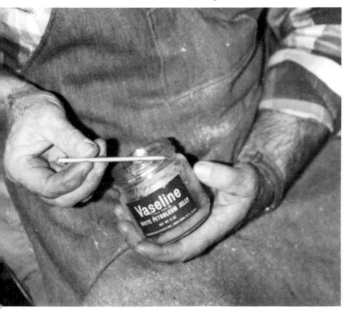

Head retention screw coated with vaseline to ensure against epoxy contamination of screw threads.

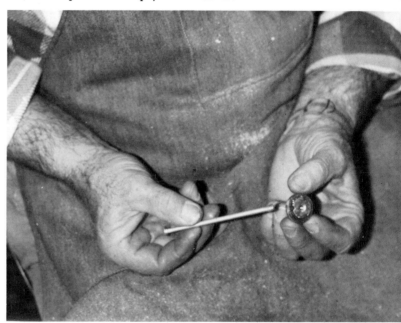

Head retention screw and plywood washer/tee nut assembly.

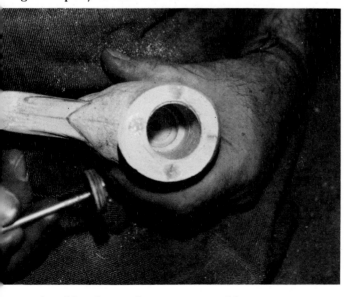

Head and head retention screw assembly.

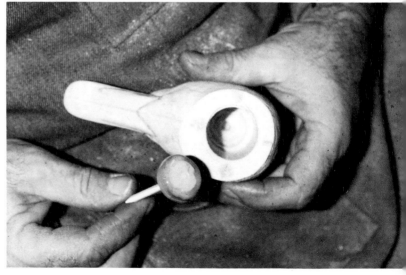

Tee nut screw assembly ready for insertion into head.
Note: Epoxy on tee nut plywood washer.

Assembly inserted into head.

Head and body. (Showing penciled areas to be relieved to ensure trouble-free joint).

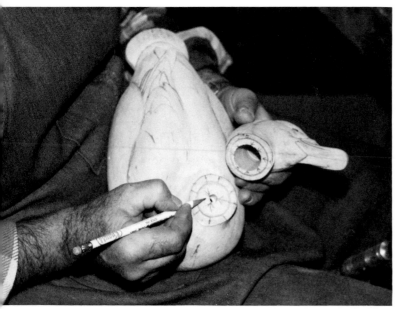

Pencil points out area to be relieved.

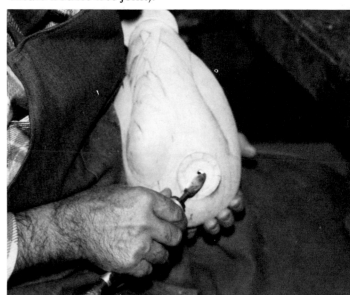

Conical cutter relieves area within circle (like a pie plate), for improved glue joint strength.

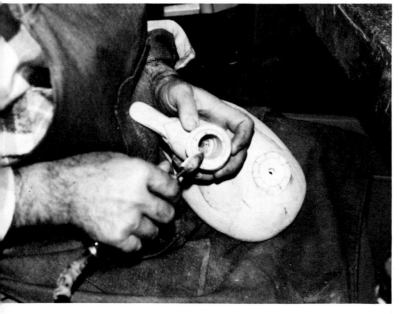

Mating area of head interface is relieved.

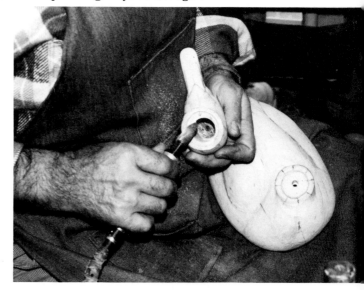

Another view. Bevel area of head bottom to form a "pie plate".

78

Epoxy is spread on body.

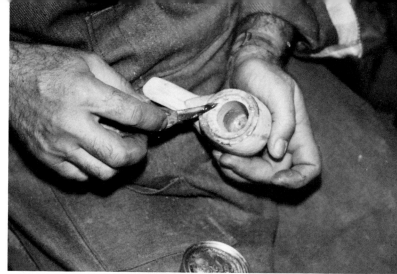

Epoxy is spread on head.

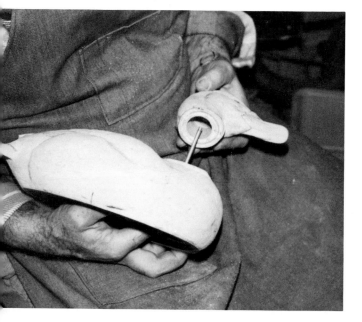

Head retention screw in place and head is readied.

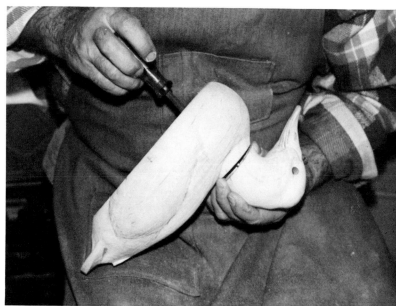

Head is positioned and secured (clamped against adhesive) with a ¼" diameter bolt going into tee nut which is secured within the hollowed head.

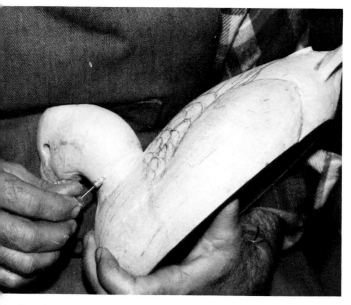

Cutting an irregular groove around "glued" joint to be filled with acetone thinned "wood dough" to mask joint.

Acetone and wood dough, brushes and tools preparatory to setting eyes and filling groove at intersection of head/body.

79

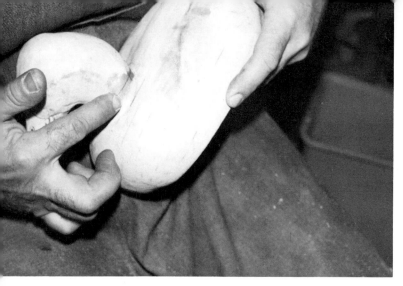

Acetone and wood dough solution applied to groove to mask head/body joint.

Saturating eye area with acetone before applying wood dough to eye hole to improve adhesion.

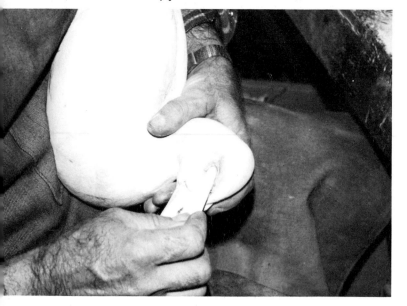

Filling in eye hole with wood dough.

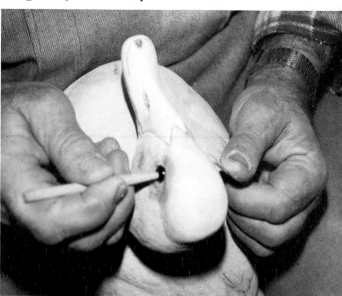

Push in eye with a dowel. Dowel end is countersunk to prevent dowel from slipping off eye to properly set depth of glass eye.

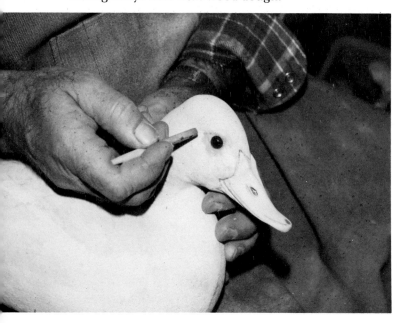

Eye depth established.

With eye depth established, cover eye completely with wood dough and start exposing eye to attain desired appearance.

Shaping eye opening with acetone saturated small #2 brush.

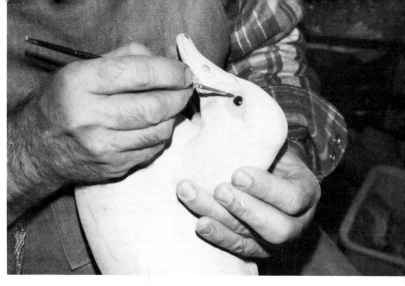

Making vee crease in front of eye with stiff #2 brush.

Shaping eye opening with acetone saturated small #2 brush.

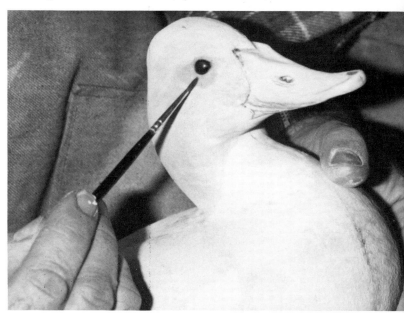

Brush on solvent to establish eye lid shape.

Epoxy (glue) joint groove is undercut in side to permit excess wall epoxy to have space and thus improve glue joint.

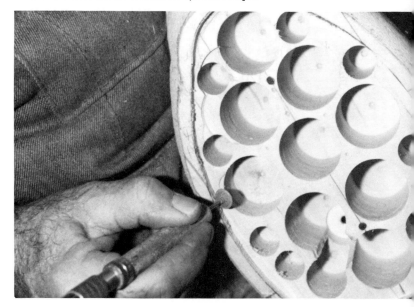

Cutting in glue relief joint in side wall using saw type shaped stone.

81

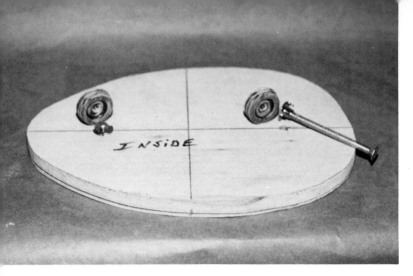

Bottom board insert tee nuts installed. ¼'' plywood caps are epoxy secured to prevent water intrusion.

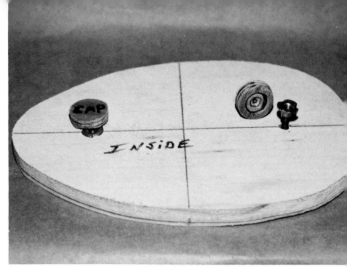

Notice ¼'' plywood caps are slightly hollowed to accomodate "T" nut and ¼-20 bolt.

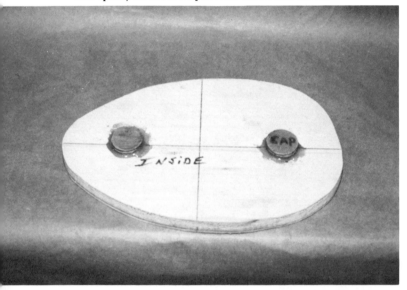

¼'' plywood caps epoxy (glued) in position. ¼'' tee nuts are sealed by these caps to prevent water intrusion.

Water filled pan and plastic sheet is used to establish preliminary balance of decoy.

Decoy with preliminary balance weight temporarily retained with rubber bands. *Note:* At this time the decoy has been colored in chest, head and rump areas with a "Deft" (mfg) lacquer compatible color stain. This gives an overall feel of the decoy and transitional areas.

Decoy floatation. *Note:* Lead is weighed on scale and then positioned inside of decoy to establish balance.

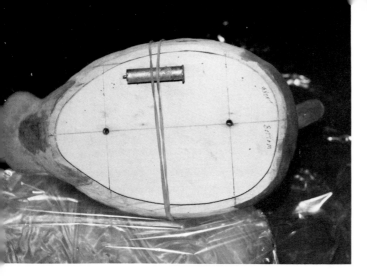

Preliminary balance.

Note: Lead (weight) was weighed and tested in tank before "gluing" in place.

Counter balance weight glued in place.

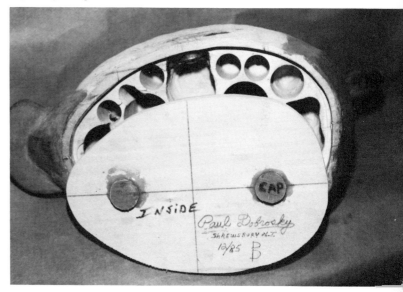

Bottom board insert ready for assembly. ¼" plywood caps "glued" over top of tee nuts.

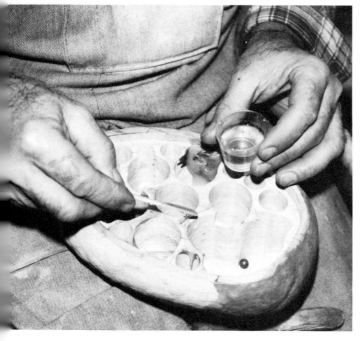

Epoxy spread for bottom board assembly.

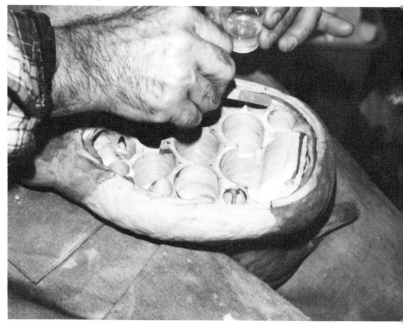

Another view.

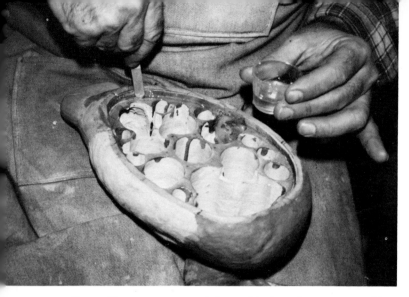

Spreading epoxy on weight and in board area recess. Also on mating facets of the bottom board.

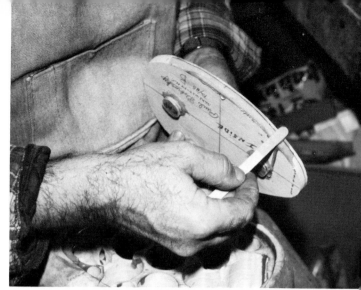

Spread epoxy on balance of inside and on bottom board.

Bottom board installed.

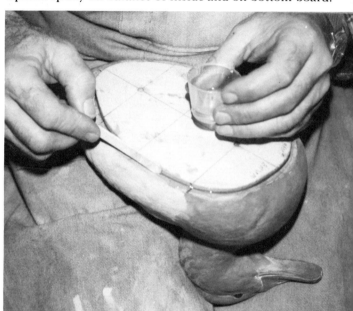

Epoxy put around seam of installed bottom board.

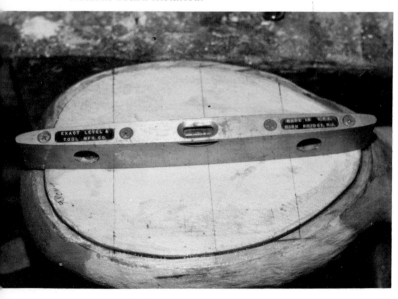

Decoy leveled in vise to ensure epoxy is retained in position while still fluid.

Mirror image as an aid to viewing decoy silhouette. Assists in review of decoys' continuity. *Note:* At this point, the carver may want to change something on the carving before final sealing.

Note: At this time the decoy has been colored in head, chest, and rump area with a Deft (mfg) lacquer compatible color stain. This gives a feel for the overall view of the decoy and transitional areas.

Note: Mirror image technique is also used throughout the painting steps.

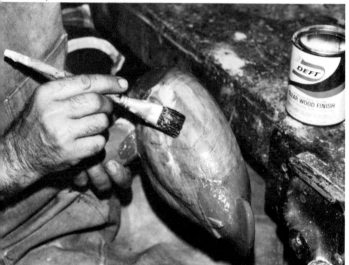

Application of wood sealer. (Deft lacquer)

Keel retention screws serve as work holder.

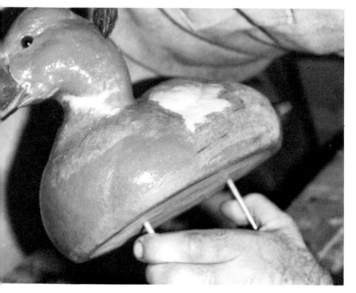

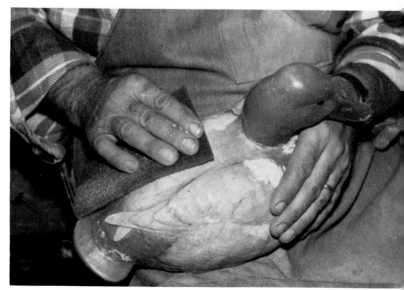

Using keel fasteners as holding fixture when applying sealer.

Sanding decoy with green scouring pad prepares surface for gesso prime coat.

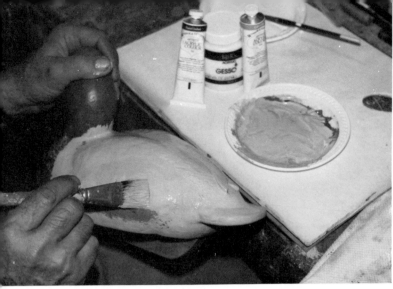

Gesso being applied. Gesso is tinted with burnt umber and cobalt blue, similar to base color of bird.

Hair dryer used to speed drying of gesso prime coat.

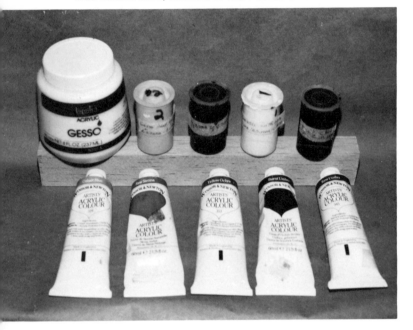

Color Layout

Transparent film canisters (Fuji film) are used to store pre-mixed colors. Gesso is used as tint and as a base coat. A paint flow improver, drying retarder and pigment dispersion medium, "floetrol" by Flood Mfg. Co. are used. Distilled water was used.

Cannister no.	Color mix	Where used
#1	Gesso with tints burnt umber, raw sienna and cobalt blue	Lightest value, base coat —back and sides
#2	Gesso, raw sienna, burnt umber and cobalt blue	Creamy color around eye, under chin and front of neck
#3	1/3 burnt umber and 2/3 raw sienna (by volume) (mixed with distilled water)	Rump, chest, (top) of head
#4	1/2 cobalt blue and 1/2 burnt umber	Darkest accent color for head and rump and chest area

By intermixing the four canister blends into at least three values (by mixing with Gesso white) continuity of color can be achieved in the "bird".

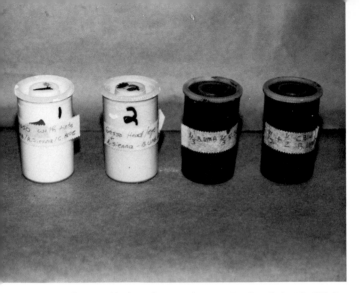

Colors to be applied (color canisters #1, #2, #3, & #4). This ensures enough pre-mixed colors to complete decoy.

The pallet for first application of base colors. *Note:* Paints are first placed on folded, water soaked paper towel with ⅛" thick, wet sponge underneath to retard drying time.

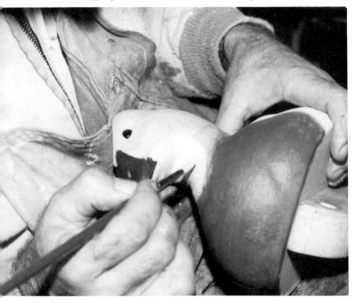

Gesso with color added, applied to light/dark areas. Painting base colors close to finish colors in various areas of bird.

Wet blending removes sharp demarcations in areas and gives soft finished look.

Paint base color on side of head.

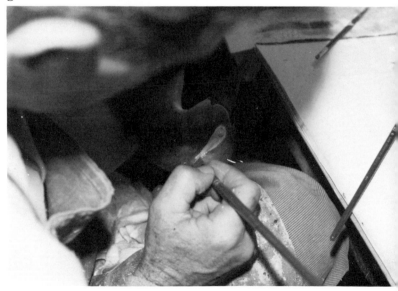

Painting in light color around eye.

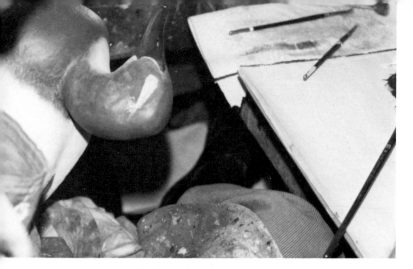

Painting in light color around eye.

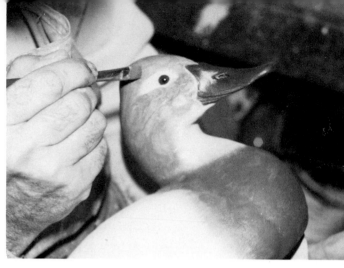

Stipple blending, dark to light areas.

Stipple blending, dark to light areas.

Painting light area in front of cheek and behind bill.

Stipple blending light to dark area.

Primary colors applied as base coat. This undercoat is the lightest value of color in chest.

88

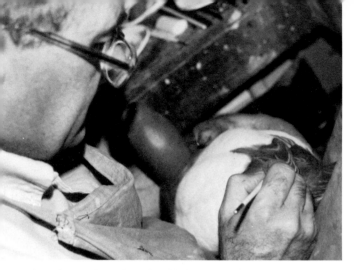

Primaries and tertials detailed. (Work back to front)

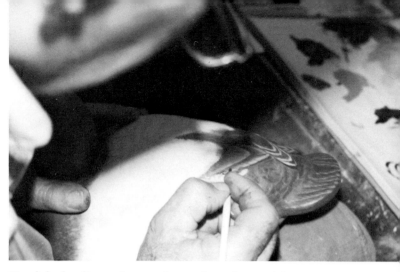

Tertial detail, various color values in tertial group feathers.

Painting tertials.

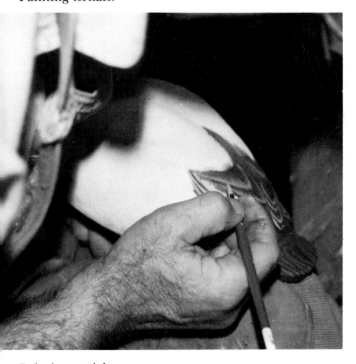

Painting tertials.

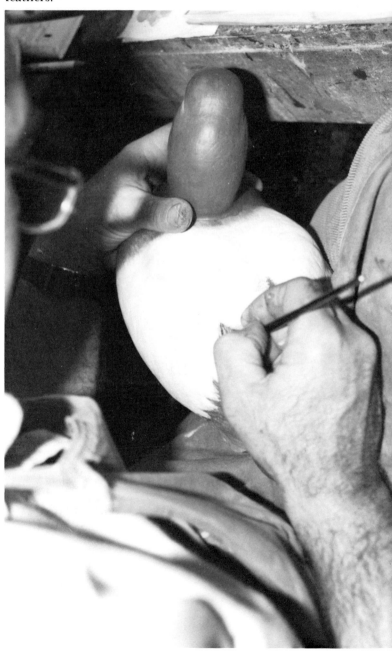

Another view of painting tertials.

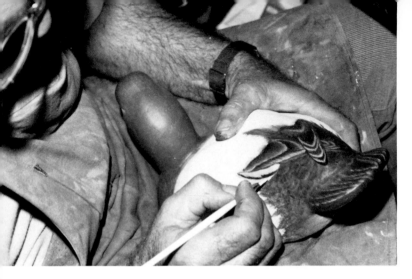

Speculum being detailed.

Painting speculum.

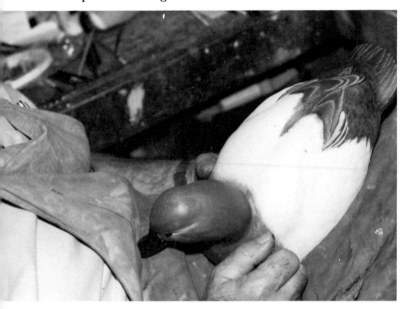

Inspection.

By painting from back to front of bird, feathers can be made to appear overlaid and softer in appearance.

Ready to paint side pocket feather groups.

Various values of dark colors painted on side feathers areas.

Harold Haman

Canada Goose

Harold Haman was born in Wilmington, Delaware on April 4th, 1932; and has been a lifelong resident of Delaware. He is retired and lives in New Castle.

Harold started hunting at the age of ten, with his father, and continues to this day to be an avid hunter and decoy maker. He has made gunning decoys for some of the large catalog houses and countless individuals.

His hunting decoys have the reputation of being extremely serviceable. They are made of cork from Portugal, with cedar heads and cedar or cyprus bottom boards.

Harold's exploits on the Delaware River and Bay are the stuff of legends. He practically "invented" lay out gunning in this area and has been written about in several magazine articles, one of which was in Petersons Hunting, entitled "LAY-OUT Rigs—The Goose Getters". This is one of the most successful methods of goose hunting anywhere.

Harold has come a long way since he started making hunting decoys at about age 21, out of necessity. Like many young hunters, he simply could not afford to buy decoys so he made them. Later, in the mid-60's, due to a severe financial crunch of heavy medical bills, Harold began a decoy business in addition to his full time job. Over the years he has made literally thousands of decoys, which uniquely qualifies him to "build one decoy", as we show here.

Harold Haman—Canada Goose

Reduced 30%

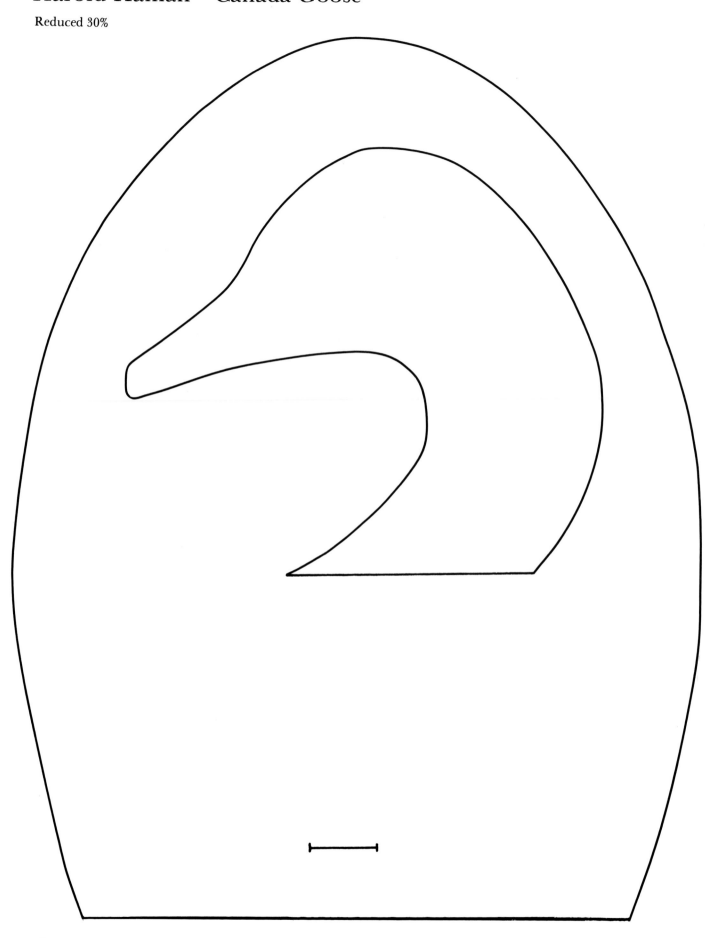

Harold Haman—Canada Goose

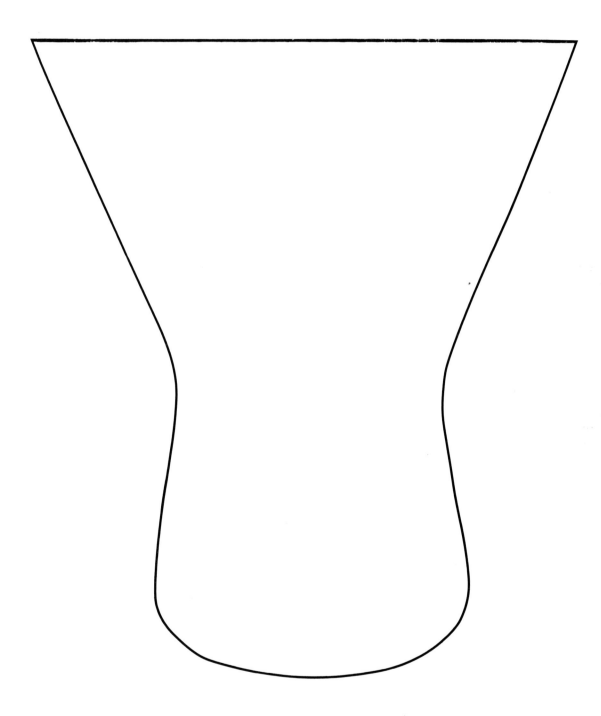

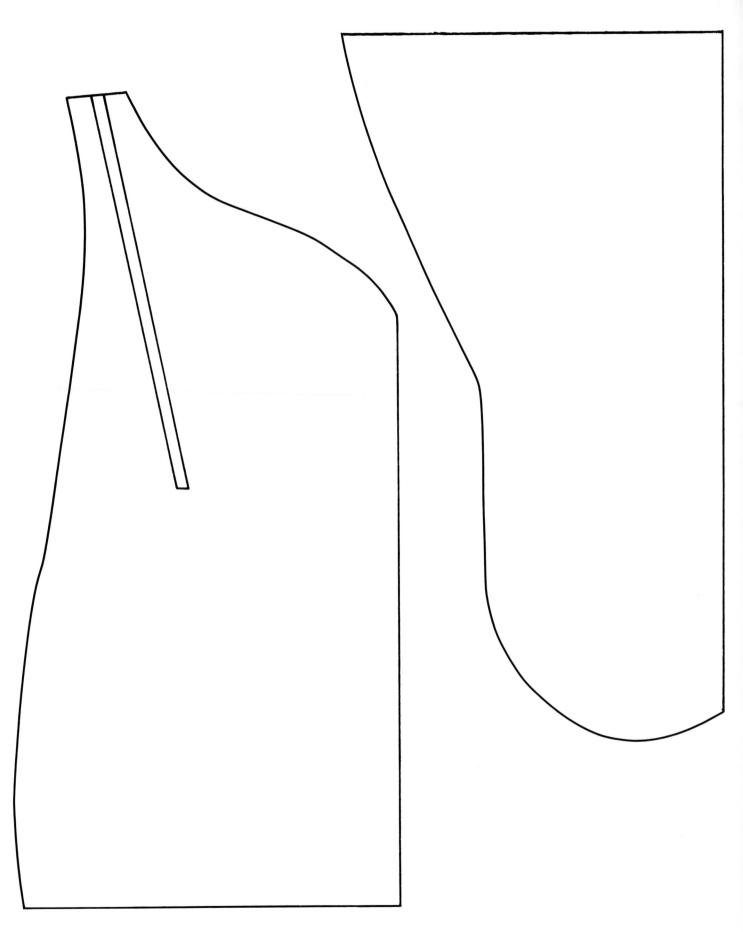

Harold Haman—Canada Goose

94

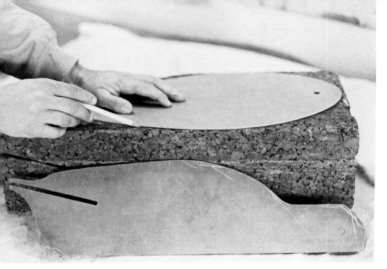

Tracing pattern onto cork (this is Portugal natural cork).

Gluing cedar bottom board onto cork.

Fiberboard insert in tail.

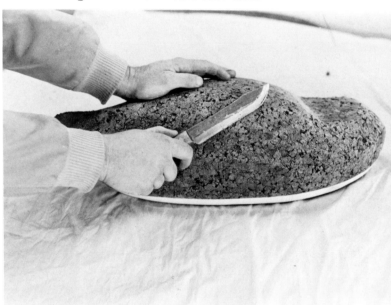

Cutting excess cord away with butchers knife.

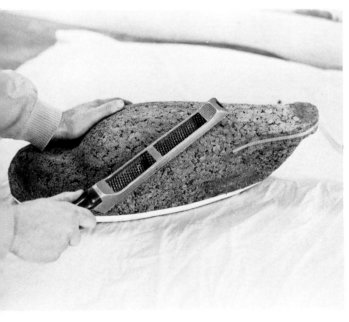

Final shaping of body with sur form rasp.

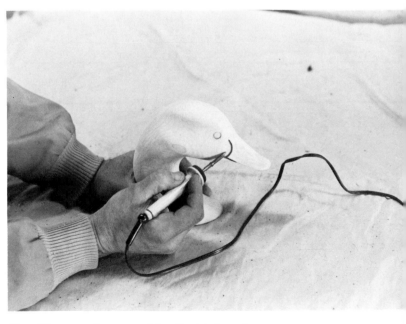

Detailing wooden carved head with burning pen.

Sanding head on 2″ drum sander.

Attaching cedar or pine keel with screws.

Head is attached with brass screw eye—(note eye is cut into head with hollow tube and painted with gloss medium over black paint).

Charlie "Speed" Joiner
Wood Duck (Hen and drake)

Charlie was born on July 19th 1921 at Betterton, Maryland. He began hunting as a youngster and was an avid hunter until the mid-1960's, at which time he quit. He is not against hunting but says he has just had enough.

Today he likes to shoot trap and skeet and travel. Charlie particularly likes to travel in the South West and appreciates the Indian artifacts. As a youngster he collected Indian artifacts along the Sassafras River.

Charlie started an apprenticeship with master decoy maker R. Madison Mitchell of Havre de Grace, Maryland in 1942, then went into the armed forces for three years. From 1946 until 1950 he returned to the Mitchell shop and became a master carver in his own right.

During the late 1950's Charlie met and was greatly influenced by the famous Ward Brothers of Crisfield, Maryland. During the late 40's he lived in Aberdeen, Maryland, making it convenient to the Mitchell shop.

In 1950 he returned to Betterton and was working for the electric company. By 1963 Charlie had moved into management and needed to be closer to his job, so he moved to Chestertown, Maryland.

Charlies says he has been half way around the world and there is no place he would rather be.

Charlie has done flat painting and is considered by many to be one of the greatest decoy painters in the country.

His work is avidly sought after by countless collectors and many of his peers also collect his work. This in itself speaks loudly on his behalf.

Charlie loves visitors and says that he is really appreciative of decoys, the interest in them and what they have contributed to him.

When asked where he got the nickname "Speed", he said that his father was so slow that people called him "Speedy", when Charlie came along it was "Big Speed" and "Little Speed".

Charlie "Speed" Joiner—Wood Duck (Hen and drake)

Full size

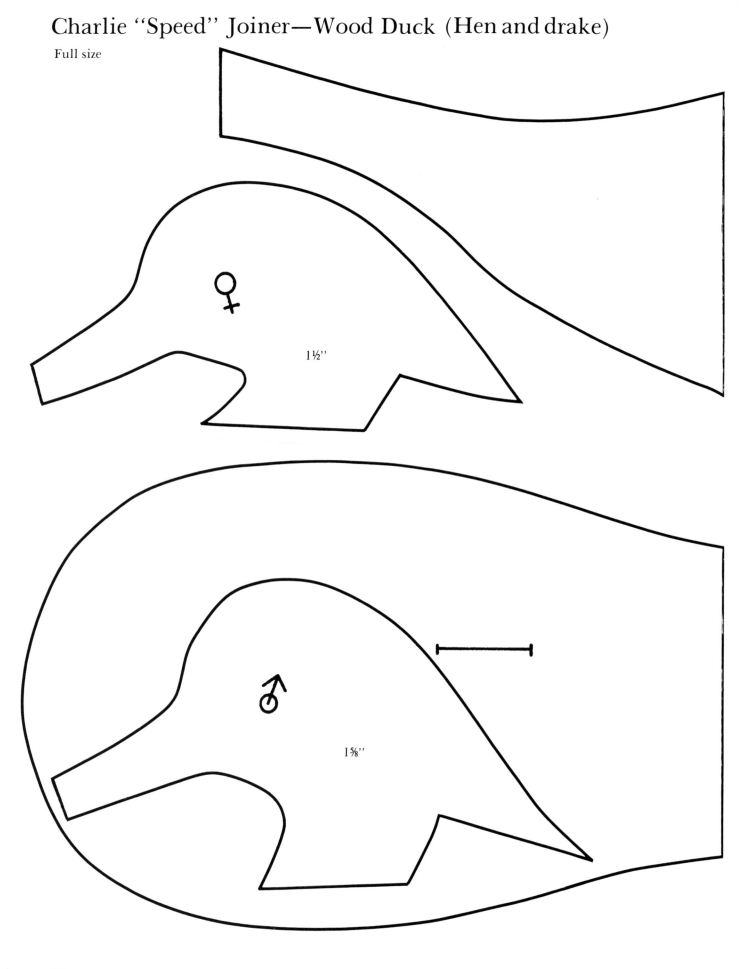

♀

1½"

♂

1⅝"

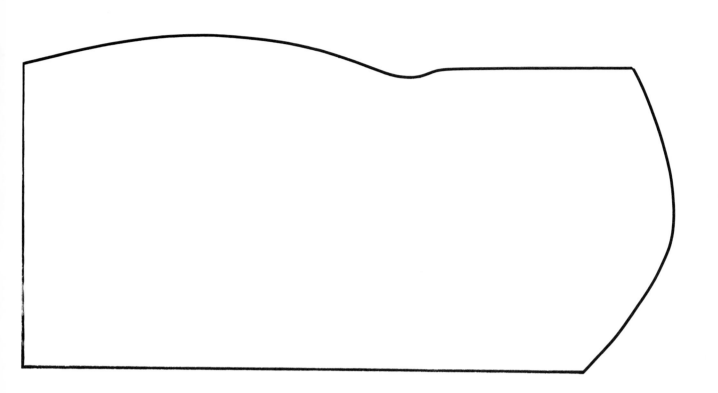

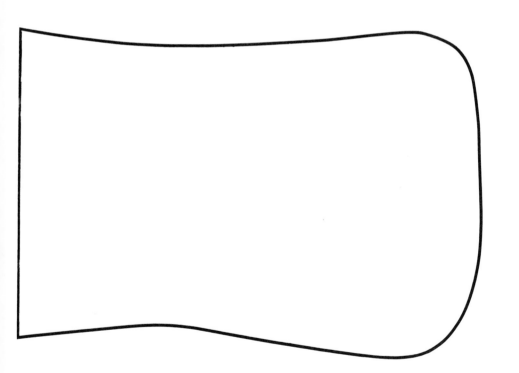

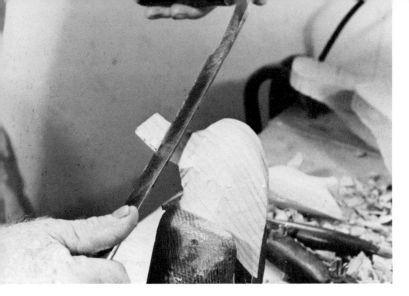

Roughing head with drawknife.

Roughing head with drawknife.

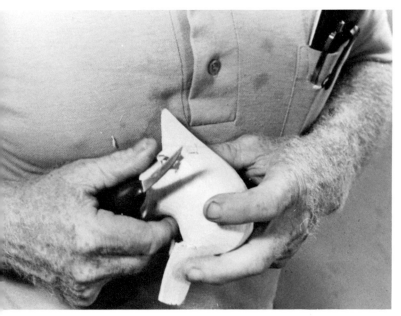

Shaping of hood with knife.

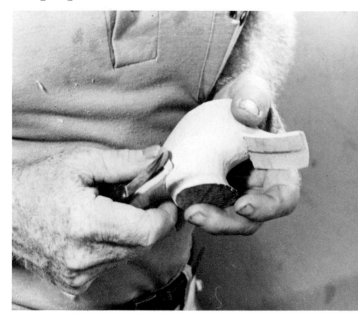

Side view of head.

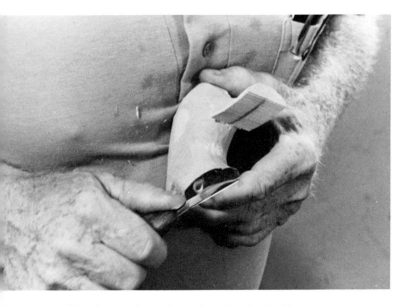

Shaping under chin and neck with knife.

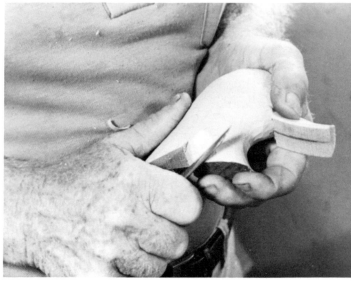

Shaping neck under hood with knife.

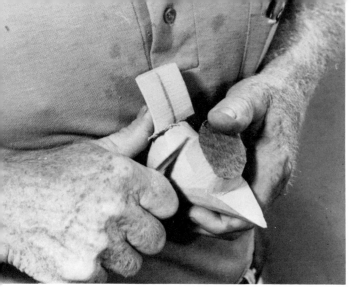

Shaping under chin.

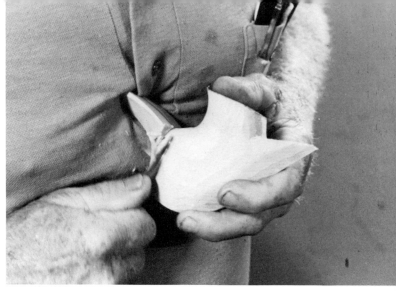

Shaping forecheek.

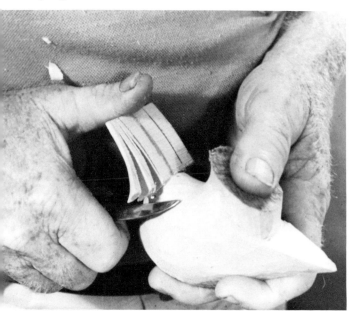

Cutting excess wood away to shape bill. Note: use pencil lines to size bill.

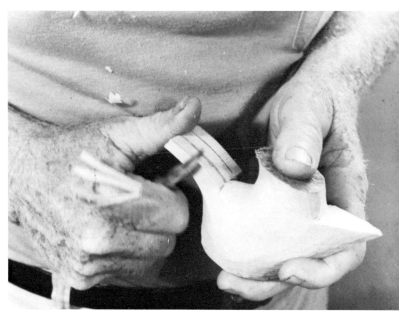

Shaping exactly on line for final size.

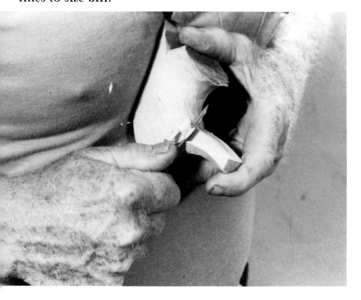

Back cut bill to head.

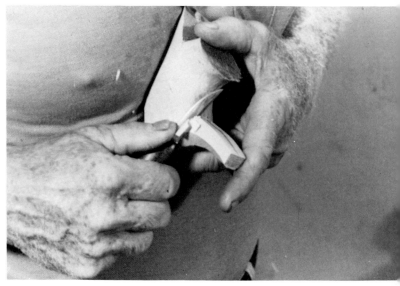

Cut from head to bill to allow smooth flow.

101

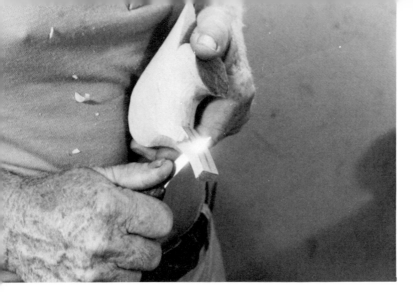

Shaping other side of bill.

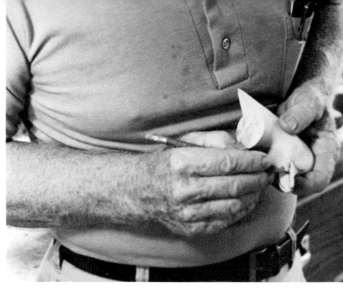

Marking bill lines for cut-in.

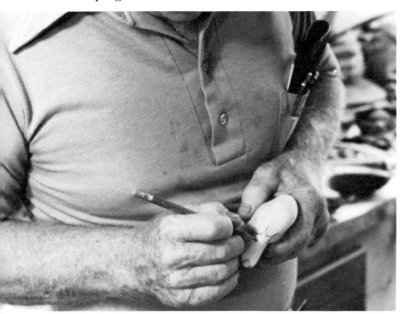

Marking nail and nostrils.

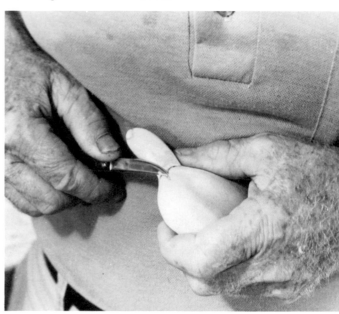

Cut in at culmen and forecrown.

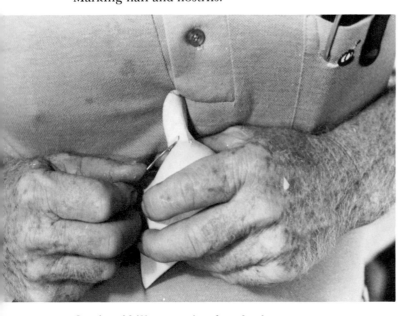

Cut in of bill separating forecheek.

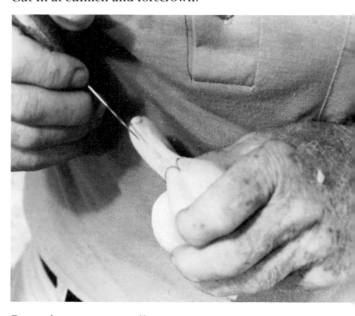

Preparing to cut nostril.

102

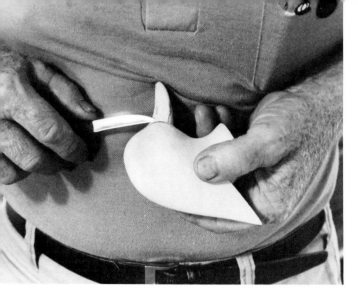

Back cut on forecheek.

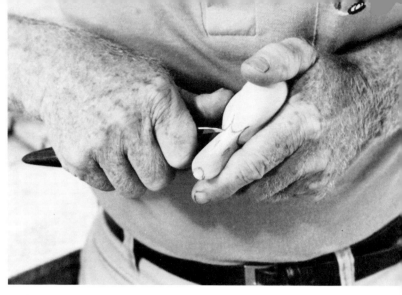

90° cut to forecheek.

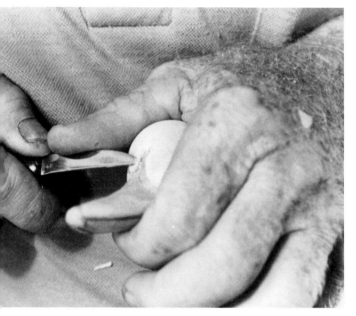

Shaping forecrown.

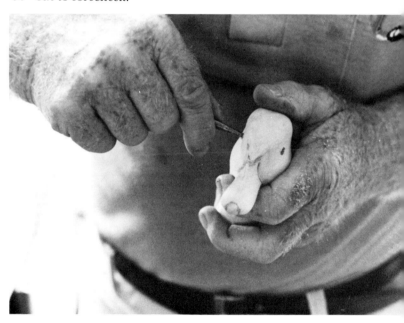

Marking eye placement.

Close up of bill detail.

Close up of underbill.

103

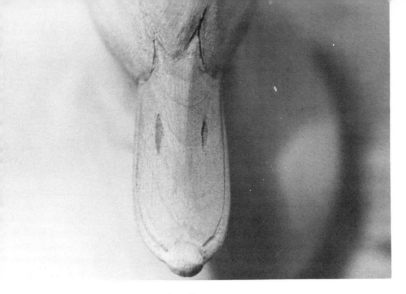
Top view of bill detail.

Drilling eye hole.

Drilling hole in neck for dowel placement.

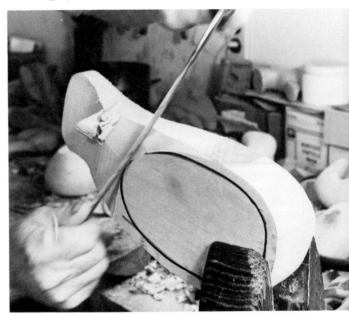
Carving under tail with drawknife.

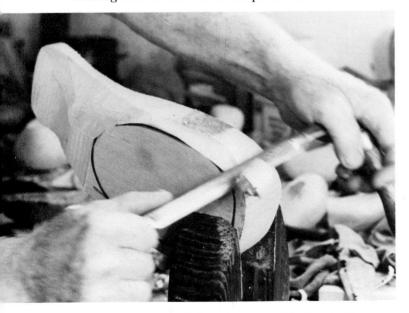
Cutting excess wood along bottom with drawknife.

Carving top of body with drawknife.

Smoothing the rough shape with spokeshave.

More spokeshave work.

Carving other side with drawknife.

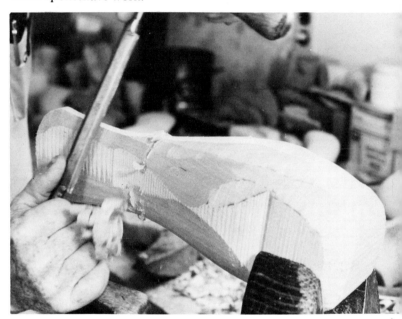

Carving upper side of tail with drawknife.

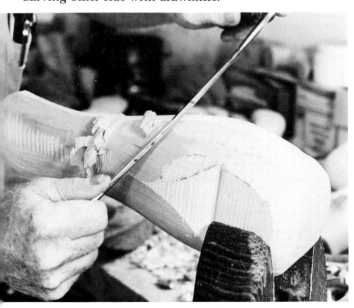

Carving body with drawknife. (note vise).

Spokeshave work on body.

Checking for balance in the carving.

Carving underside of tail with drawknife.

Shaping chest with sur form rasp. (This is a flat blade some carvers use curved blade.)

Further shaping with sur form rasp.

Smoothing chest with spokeshave.

Smoothing under tail with spokeshave. (Note: the spokeshave makes a very fine cut, many old time carvers used a spokeshave instead of sanding.

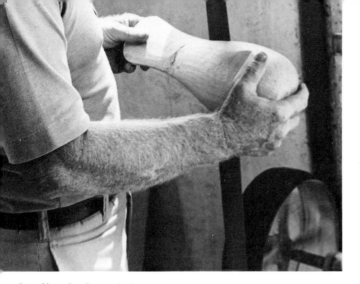

Sanding body on belt sander.

Sanded body—note center line.

Indentation on back is cut in with hatchet. (Hatchet is razor sharp.)

Final cutting of indentation with hatchet.

Ragged edges cut with knife.

Sanding indentation by hand with 80 grit paper.

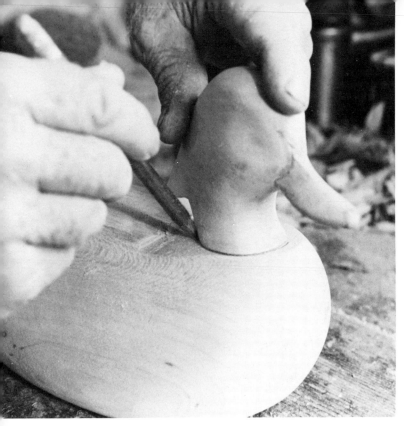

Positioning head.

Position of head—note outer mark—it is ascertained by chalking drilled hole in head which is then transferred to body.

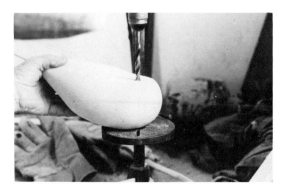

Drilling dowel hole.

Marking drill center hole.

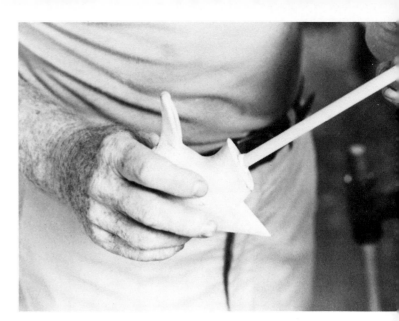

Gluing dowel rod in head.

Shaping chest to head area.

Gluing dowel in body and positioning head.

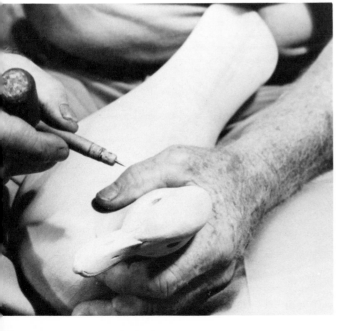

Special tool for punching hole deep in center of eye hole to accommodate longer eye wire. This insures greater strength in setting eyes.

Neck joint filled with plastic wood and sanded.

Head ready to set eyes.

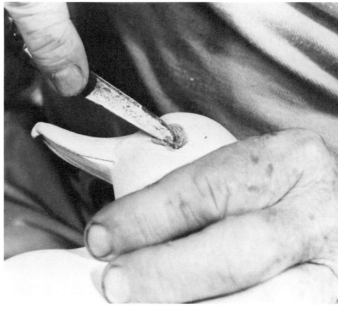

Fill eye hole with plastic wood and set eyes.

Ned Mayne

Red Head

Bordered by the Atlantic Ocean and the Delaware and Chesapeake Bay lies the Del-Mar-Va Penninsula, one of the richest waterfowl wintering areas in the world. Ned Mayne grew up amidst the numerous creeks, rivers, marshes and grain fields there and quickly gained a keen awareness of waterfowl and their habitat.

As a youngster he absorbed the expertise of his elders whom he accompanied on his earliest gunning trips. A youthful interest in taxidermy provided a sound background knowledge of waterfowl anatomy.

Ned later received his B.A. degree in Art from the University of Delaware. Military duty in Europe presented the opportunity to regularly study the old masters in France, Italy, and the Netherlands.

In addition to painting, Ned Mayne has devoted much of his time to carving both working and decorative competition decoys. He has won awards at the U.S. National Decoy Show at Babylon, New York, The Greater Snow Goose Decoy Contest at Chincoteague, Virginia, and the Ward Foundation World Championships.

Most recently, in 1980, Ned was honored by having his entry selected as the winning design for the First Delaware Duck Stamp Contest.

His interest in making decoys was created out of necessity. He could not afford gunning decoys, so he made them and turned that job into fun. Now residing in Wilmington, Delaware, Ned is single and has no intention of changing this status because it may interfere with his hunting and fishing.

I have had my best luck in changeable weather. When a front moves in (in a hurry), look for your best success. On blue bird days the most skilled hunter with the better rig location and more lifelike decoys generally will do best. On these days, layout gunning on big water seems to be good. Harold Haman and Ned Mayne in this book are experts in this type of hunting. As in all wildfowl hunting, a good man behind a call will do wonders. Also, don't forget, a good rig of full bodies and silhouettes will also work, given a chance in the right weather. Sometimes, any movement of decoys, black flags or even a dog will attract distant ducks. Be extremely still when ducks are close for they are not color blind and any motion attracts their attention."

Ned Mayne—Red Head

Full size

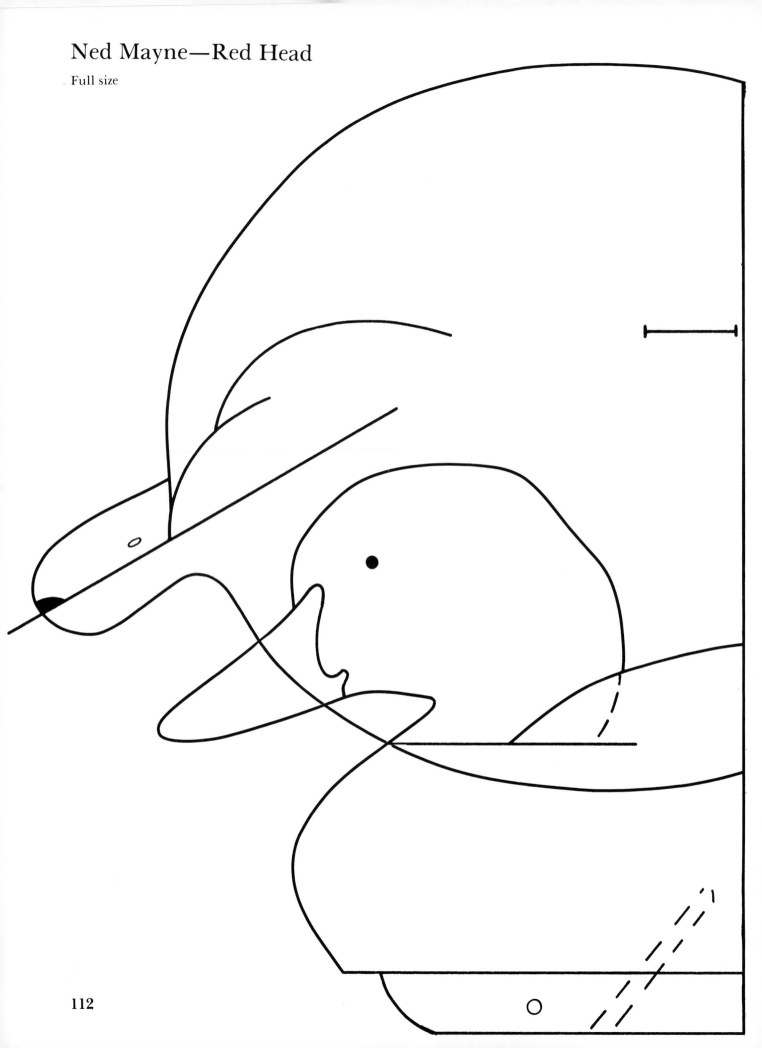

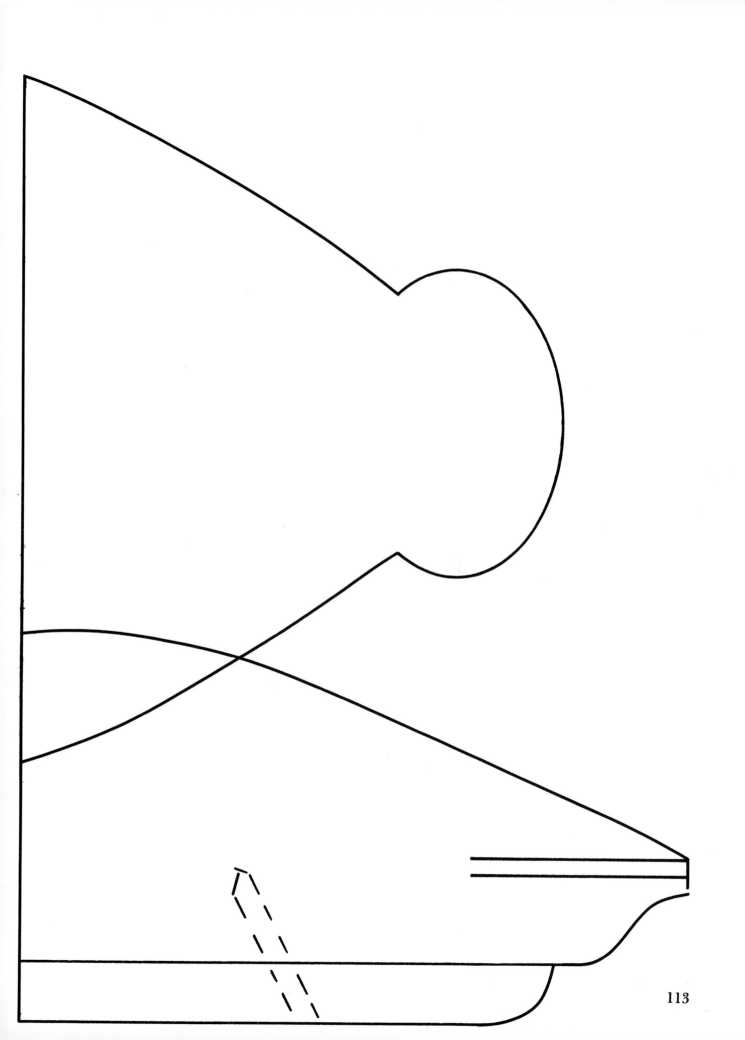

113

Cork block glued up, ready to be band-sawed. (This is high density Wiley cork.)

Body is band-sawed and is being trimmed.

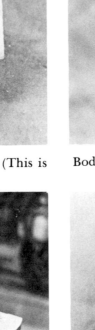

Further trimming.

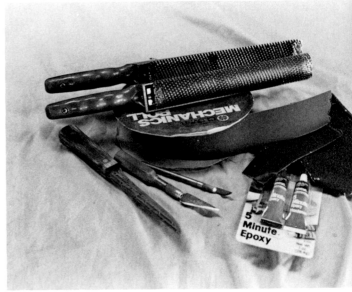

Basic tools for carving decoy with cork body and wooden head.

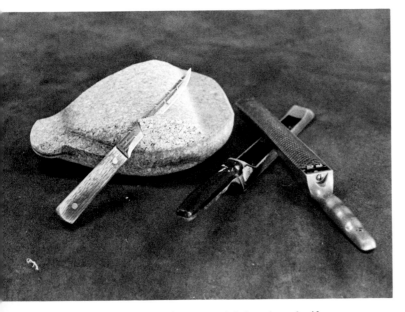

Cutting excess cork away with butchers knife.

Shaping body with sur form rasp.

114

Body basically shaped with keel in place—note fiberboard insert in tail for strength.

Another view.

Head carved.

Head being fitted to body and dowel being placed for strength.

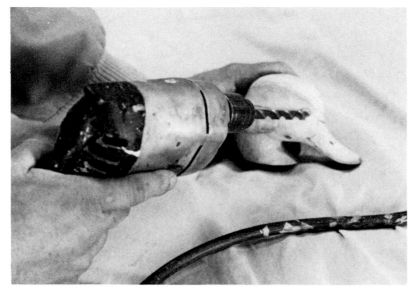

Eye hole being drilled for yellow 10mm eye. Head is then set and decoy is ready to paint.

Terry McNulty
Pintail

Terry McNulty resides in Medford, New Jersey with his wife, Peggy, and two of his four daughters. He grew up in Riverside, New Jersey, which sits along the Delaware River and is quite famous for it's decoys. Men who hunted and lived along the River (affectionately called River Rats) carved their own decoys which have become very collectible. Delaware River birds are known for their sleek styling, hollow bodies, raised primaries and detailed feather paint. Much detail went into the decoys because many of the

men sculled the ducks. In sculling, the decoys are placed away from the land in hopes that the ducks will settle in with them. If your decoys look too alert or don't ride well in the water, the ducks won't bother to stay. While the ducks are getting acquainted with your decoys, you quietly scull down the River in your boat, getting as close as possible, forcing the ducks into the air. It takes a lot of skill to close in on them. As much as he enjoys sculling, he also likes to blind hunt with his Lab, Dillon.

After several seasons of painting and making repairs to his commercially made plastic and wooden gunning decoys, Terry decided to try his hand at making his own rig. As time went by and his decoys improved, he was encouraged to enter the Ward Show in Salisbury, Maryland. The only decoy he had available was a hunting decoy, a Hen Mallard, but he took it down anyway and to his surprise, won a third place in the decorative division.

Since that time he has won numerous blue ribbons and thirteen (13) Best in Shows, including the Lem & Steve Ward Shootin' Stool contest at the World in 1985, the U.S. Nationals in New York, the Pacific Flyway Pairs Contest and the Ohio Decoy Collectors and Carvers Contest.

"Carving represents to me the link to the outdoors, being close to nature. Through carving, I can give life and character to a piece of wood. What I like best about carving hunting decoys, is that it is not an exact science. You can go for realism, but use an artistic approach to the point of accentuating a feather, enlarging the eyes or head, etc.," relates Terry. "While I do not carve for this reason, I believe that immortality becomes a by-product of this art form."

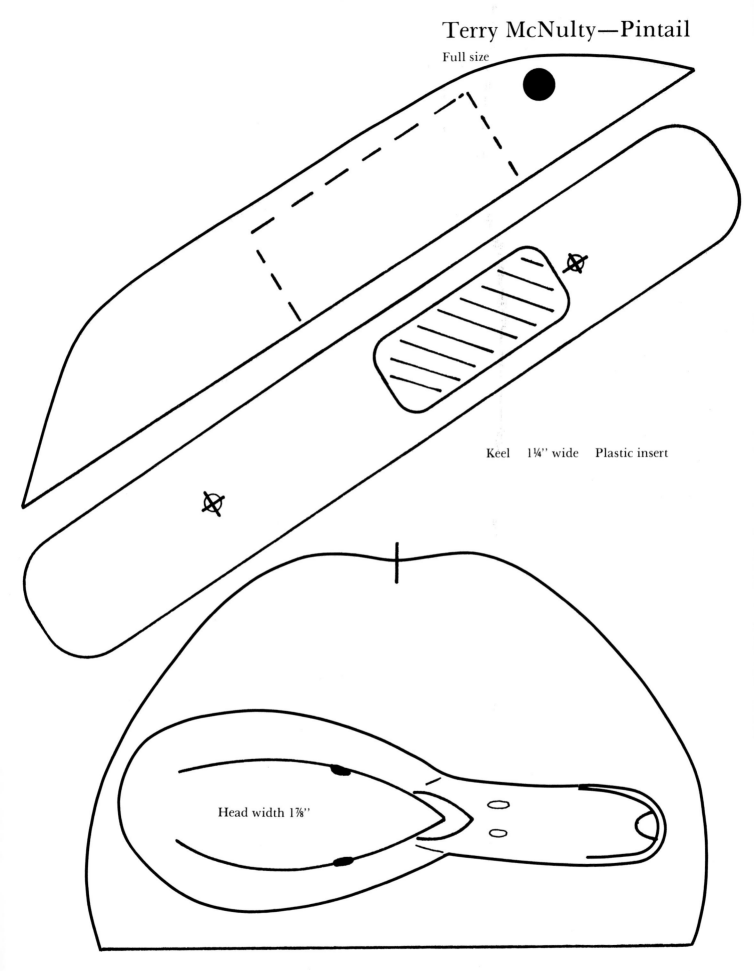

Full size

Keel   1¼'' wide   Plastic insert

Head width 1⅞''

Terry McNulty—Pintail

Full size

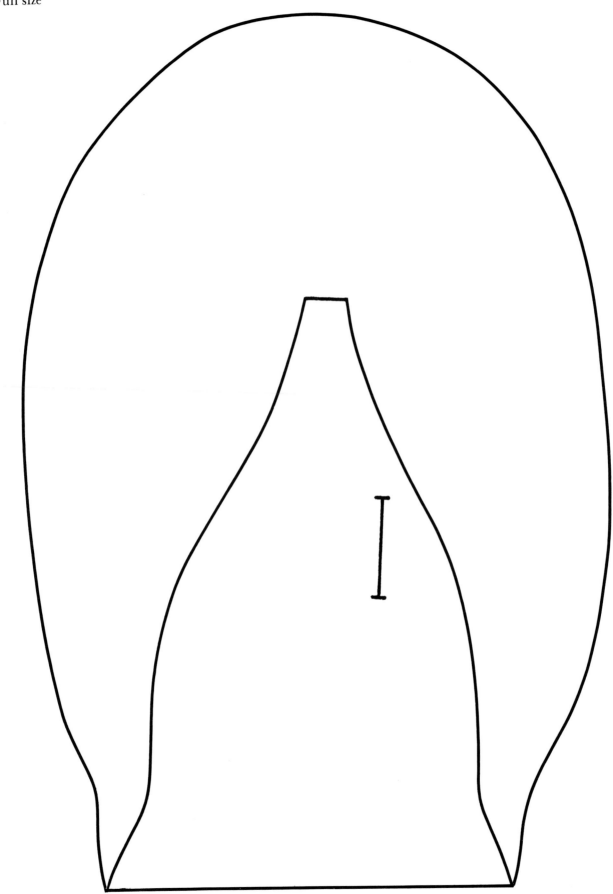

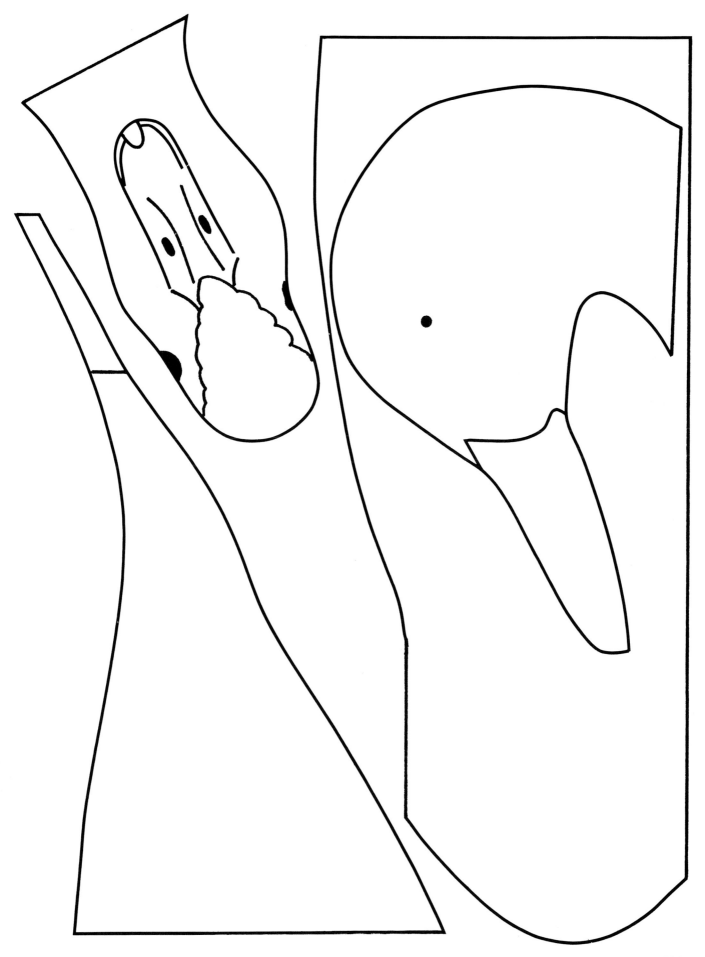

119

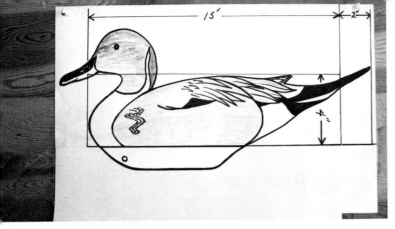

After deciding the species to be carved, the dimensions of the decoy must be decided. Bearing in mind that a hunting decoy must be at least lifesize or larger, we begin by drawing the profile, in this particular case, the Pintail Drake.

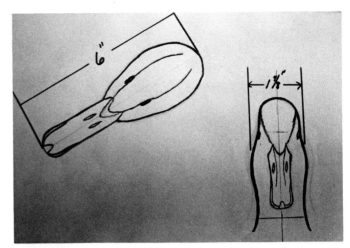

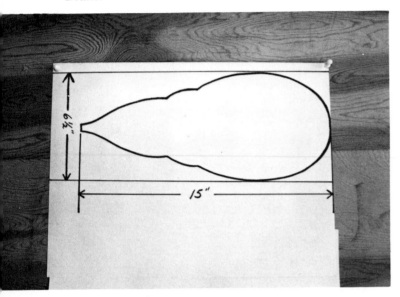

When drawing the body pattern, start by deciding the length and width, drawing what will appear to be an oblong box. Staying within those dimensions, draw the body shape. Repeat these steps for your height and width profile. You will now have the three views that will be necessary for your Pintail body.

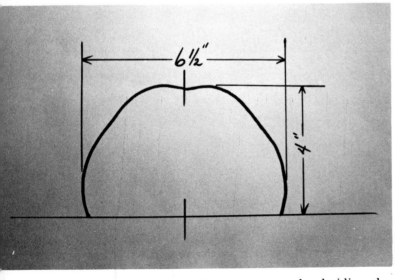

We repeat these steps, giving us the same views for our head pattern. Referring to Fig. 2a and 2b, it will be equally important to adjust the head to the body separately so that you can move it around until you are satisfied with the continuity of the head and chest. I personally like to move the head around to double check that I am giving the duck the attitude that I originally intended.

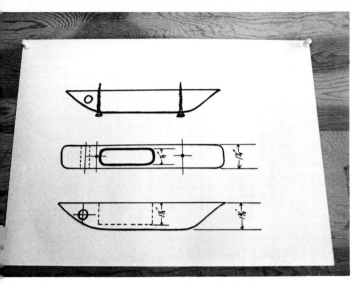

The most important part of the keel will be the placement of the lead. In a puddle duck such as the Pintail, you will want the decoy to carry it's tail high in the water, so the lead should be placed towards the front of the keel. The length of the keel will be equal to the bottom of the decoy. See Fig. 1a or 2b.

One of the most important tools to good decoy making is having a good pattern to start with. If it isn't in the pattern to begin with, it most likely won't be in the finished product. So take time with your patterns. Read them and understand what you are about to do or attempting to do. Don't be afraid to adjust or draw several patterns taking the best and most practical ideas from each one in coming up with your final plans. Remember that it takes a lot to fool a real duck. Never lose sight of the fact that a good hunting decoy has high visibility, rides well in the water and most important, is durable. The satisfaction of hunting over your own stools will be the reward for your time and patience.

Draw your pattern on the wood, keeping in mind that you would like the glue joint (Fig.6) not to be too high in the tail or too close to the head and neck platform. Also bear in mind that you would like the seam high enough that it is above the water line. Remember that your decoy could be in the water for as long as ten (10) hours a day.

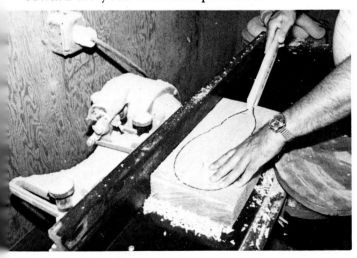

We are now ready to begin our carving. Take two (2) blocks of wood, 16'' or 17'' long with a total height of at least 4½''. Run these blocks of wood over the jointer so that they will fit together nicely.

Screw or tack-glue your wood together.

Band saw your pattern out, removing all excess wood.

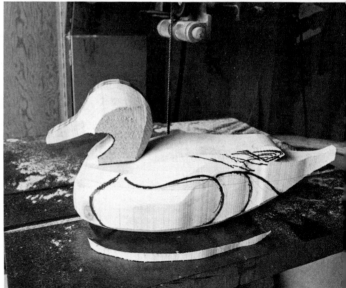

With a little skill, you can rough cut, with a Band Saw or a hatchet, all excess wood.

Mount a fastening block with long screws to the base of your decoy. This will enable you to hold and move the body around in a vise.

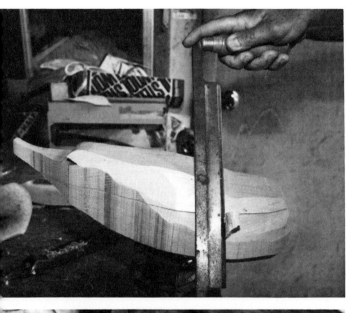
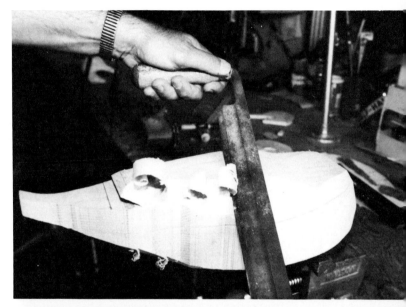

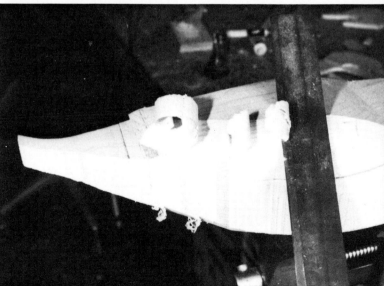

Using a draw knife, we begin to shape the body, moving to different angles in the vise.

123

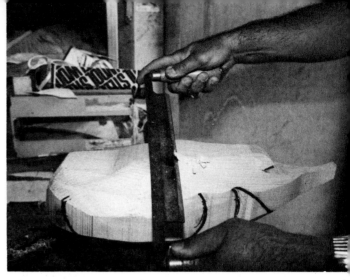

Don't be afraid to continue to draw lines and sketch on your duck. This will give you a better idea of where you can expect the flanks, primaries, etc. to be.

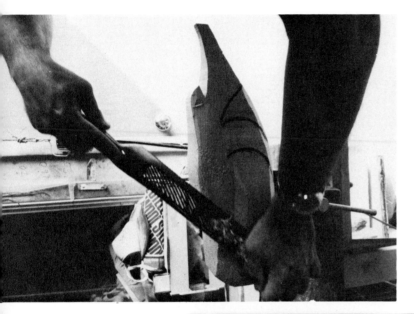

As you get closer to the final shaping you might use the Stanley Wood Rasp.

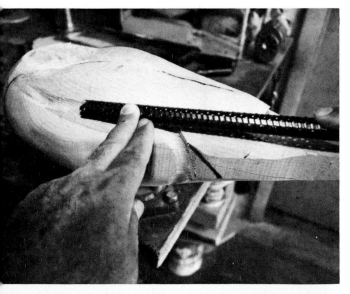

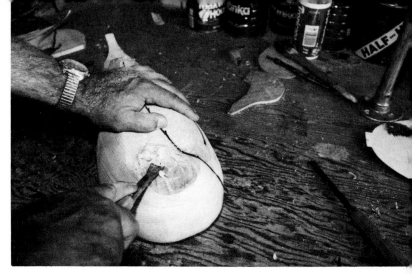

Using a gouge or chisel, prepare the platform for the head.

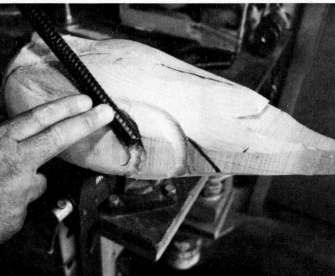

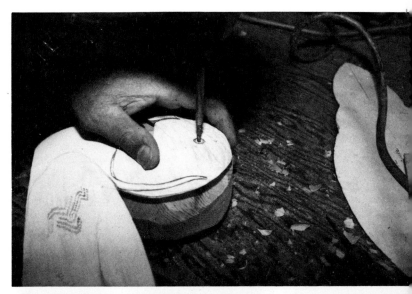

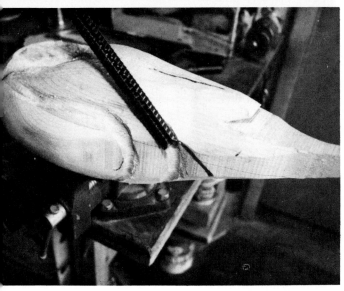

Using a Round Surform rasp, groove your flanks into the body.

Place the pattern against the head and mark the eye. Place the head on a flat surface and using a drill press and a long shank bit, drill a small hole completely through. By using this technique, your eyes should be located in the same place on both sides of the head.

125

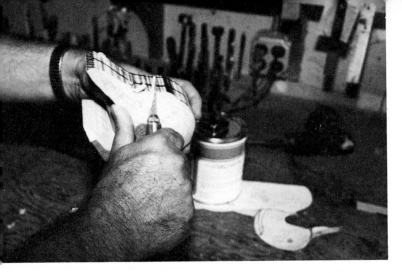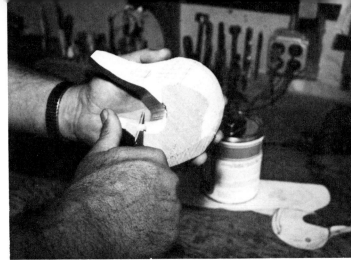

Using a sharp knife, you may begin to carve and shape the head.

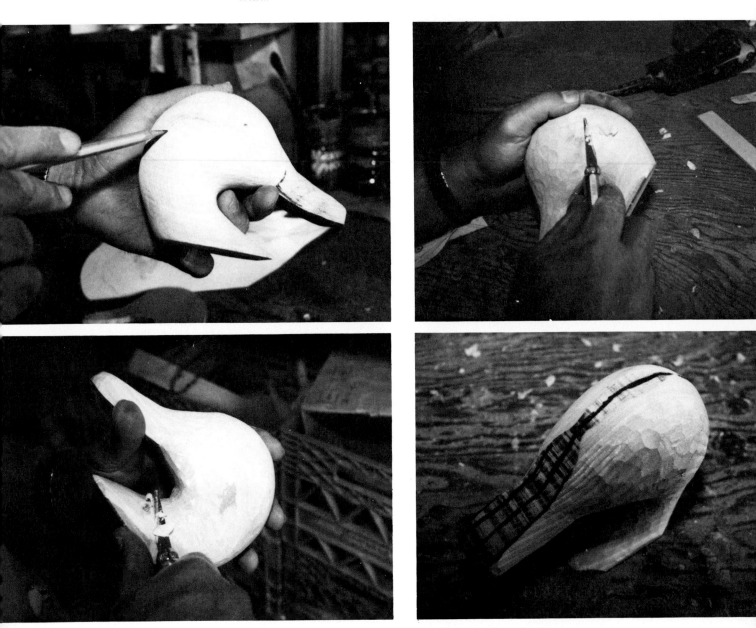

Draw pencil lines to show the flow of the feathers in the head. This will help you understand what you are trying to achieve as you whittle the excess away.

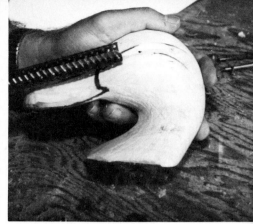

Use the wood rasp to shape and define the eye groove.

Continue to draw guide lines on the wood. By marking the underside of the bill, I know how much wood remains to be removed.

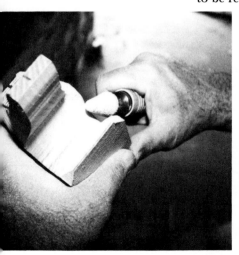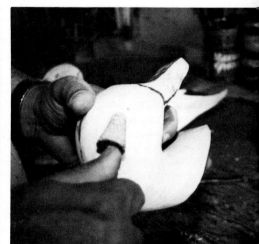

A faster way of shaping your head for those who have a Foredom Tool.

127

Using a small gouge, the nostrils are put into the bill.

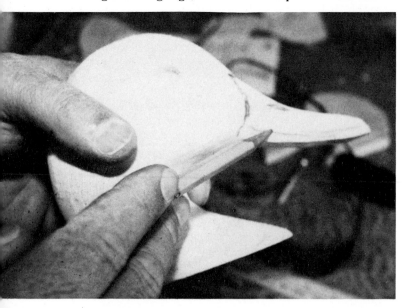

Sketching on the bill.

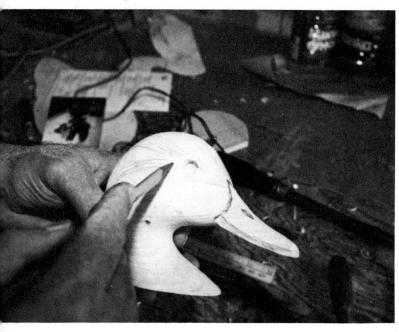

As I near the completion of the head, I continue to draw lines to guide me.

Enlarge the pilot hole for the eye to approximately the same diameter as the glass eye to be used. On a hunting decoy the head is the life of the duck. I recommend a slightly larger eye than called for to increase the lifelike attitude. Use plastic wood to fill the hole and place the glass eye in the hole. Firmly push the eye into the socket being careful to push both the right and left sides of the head in equally. You may now clean the excess away.

A good hunting decoy will not have a head too alert and yet will not have its bill tipped towards the water. Probably the most important step in having a contented decoy will be the proper placement of the head onto the body.

128

It is better to remove the wood in thin layers with a gouge and to set the head on the body so that you may achieve the proper continuity.

As with the head, continue drawing lines on the body. I refer to these lines as flow lines. They will indicate the flow of the feathers, where the feathers go, and also, will define the colors to be used at the time of painting. As our carving begins to take shape, we must be giving more and more thought to painting.

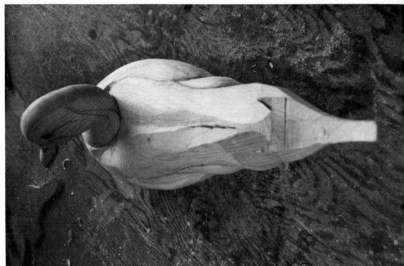

Continue to work and shape your duck.

Mount the head onto the body by first drilling a pilot hole up through the upper part of the body and head. Place Tuf-Carv between the body and head and screw a 3'' wood screw up through the head.

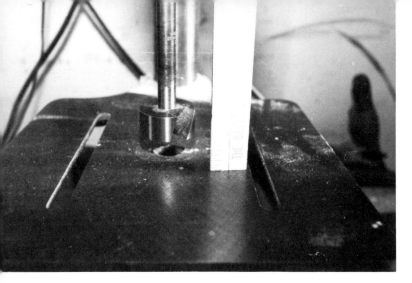

By adjusting my Drill Press to a ½", I will be able to bore my block to the proper depth.

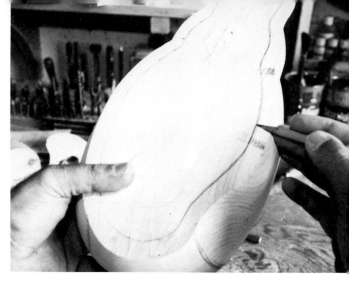

Mark off the area to be removed a ½" wall will be sufficient for a sturdy and lightweight hunting decoy.

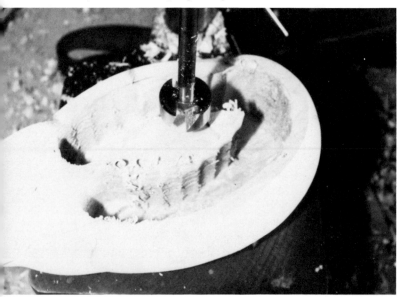

With a Forstner bit, remove excess wood.

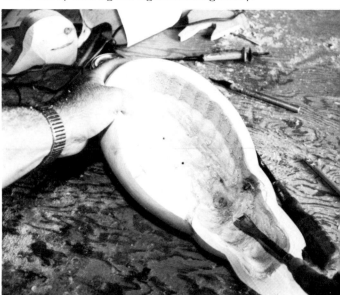

Clean out the cavity with a gouge.

While less hollowing is needed for the upper part of the body, more skill and concentration will be required due to the contours on the outer side of the carving.

With waterproof plastic resin glue, we now bond the upper and lower parts of the body together.

130

Place your decoy in a "C" clamp applying moderate pressure. You may use a piece of rubber between the decoy and clamp for protection.

Mark off the groove for your flexible plastic tail. Take a small coping saw and cut a slot approximately ⅝" into the tail.

Using plastic garden edging, cut (2) strips approximately 6" long and ½" at its widest end, tapering off to a point. Insert in the slot of the tail using a small amount of Tuf-Carv. Now drill a ⅛" hole completely through the tail inserting a ⅛" dowel. Allow to dry. Trim and sand.

Shape the lids of the eye with plastic wood filler. Using it's solvent will help keep the filler soft and pliable. You may smooth with a small brush.

After drawing the primaries, take a sharp knife and carve durable feathers into the body. These will add more realism to your carving while virtually being indestructible. After carving and a light sanding, you may clean and sharpen the edges by gently applying a hot tool to these areas.

Drill the mounting holes in your keel.

Hollow the keel for lead with a ⅝" wood bit.

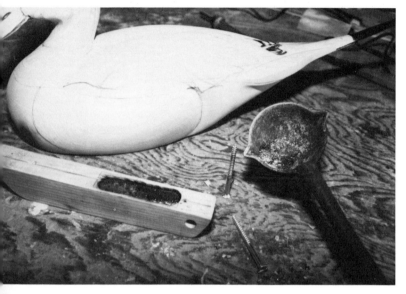

Fill cavity with melted lead.

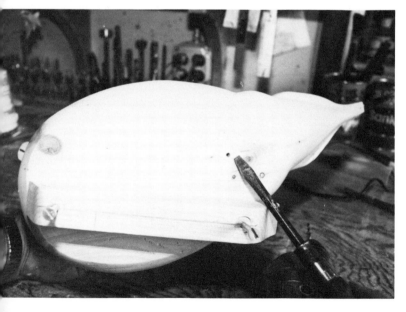

Place the keel in the appropriate spot on the body. Using a nail, mark your holes. Now drill pilot holes into the bottom of the body. This will eliminate splitting. You may now permanently attach the keel to the decoy.

Draw additional lines and sketch your feather pattern. You should be reassured that all wood has been removed and flow and continuity are evident through the entire carving.

132

The carving is completed. Be proud of your work by identifying it. Unfortunately many of the great craftsmen before us had failed to do so, leaving many fine works behind unidentified, "Carver Unknown."

Lay out your feather patterns.

Mix Hyplar Modeling Paste with gesso to the consistency of a creamy milk shake.

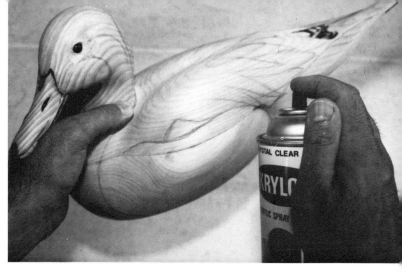

Seal your decoy with Krylon Crystal Clear 1301.

Vermiculation will be made by adding wavy lines with a metal comb.

Apply the modeling paste and gesso mixture to one side of the decoy at a time.

Working very quickly, make continuous zig-zag lines in the wet paste from the middle of the decoy and down one side. Now do the other side. This technique will require practice, but for hunting decoy vermiculation it will produce speedy results.

Painting Chart

MAB LATEX EXTERIOR		ACRYLIC
	HEAD	
Chestnut brown and black. For a darker brown, mix some black into it.	Forehead	Burnt umber, raw umber, burnt sienna, black
Chestnut brown and white	Cheek	Raw umber and white
Chestnut brown and black	Back of head	Burnt umber and black
Metal gray, ultramarine blue, black	Bill	Payne's gray, white, ultramarine blue and black
White	Neck patch	White
	BODY	
White, stipple with lambswool	Chest	White, stipple with raw umber
Comb with gesso, wash with black	Sides	Comb with gesso, wash with black
Black, metal gray, white. Wash with raw umber	Tertials	Black, gray, white. Wash with raw umber
Black, lambswool	Rump	Black, white, yellow ochre
Black and white	Tail	Black, white
Chestnut brown, white, lambswool, edge with white	Primaries	Raw umber, white and yellow ochre, edge with white

Once the paste has dried on both sides, you will apply a thinned-down wash of black paint on the entire vermiculated area.

The purpose of this chart is merely to state the colors needed to paint the Pintail Drake hunting decoy. These colors are not necessarily the only colors that may be used, but are the colors I prefer to achieve my style. It is too difficult to establish exact amounts. Many of the colors are not mixed in advance to achieve a particular color, but are mixed as I go along in a stippling and blending technique to achieve different color values, which will give depth and life to your carving.

Now take 4/0 steel wool and rub the high spots off the decoy.

134

Frank Muller

Currituck Swan and Goose

Born in Collingdale, Pennsylvania in 1942, Frank moved, with his family, to Cecil County, Maryland at 6 years of age. Growing up around waterfowlers stimulated his interest in hunting which stimulated an interest in decoys.

Working decoys were made at first for several years and then he tried some decorative birds. Realizing that there was much to learn about carving and painting techniques, he sought help and started studying with Bill Veasey.

Developing a good style enabled him to win numerous awards in New York, Maryland, Delaware, and Virginia competition for decorative and working decoys. His carvings are now located all across the United States and overseas in Germany, Great Britian, and Japan.

Frank has been a Ducks Unlimited committee member for the last 5 years and is a donor to several chapters.

Frank got interested in the Currituck, North Carolina canvas style birds while on vacation on the Currituck Sound, Outer Banks area several years ago and learned how to make the birds from decoy maker and hunter, Norman Jessup, who lives and hunts on the Currituck Sound.

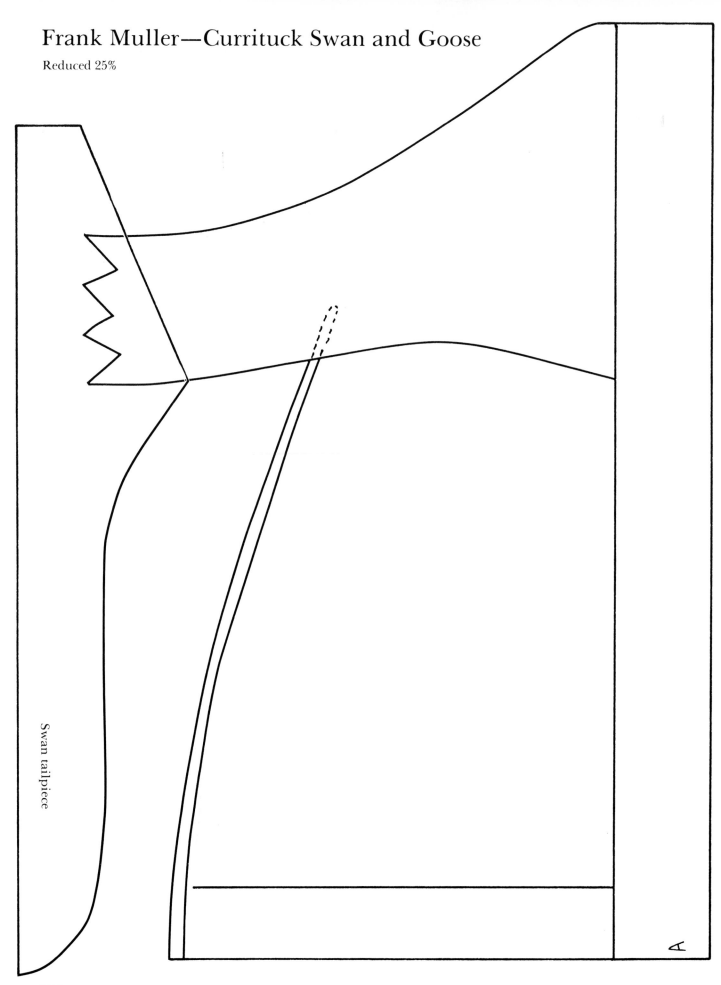

Swan tailpiece

A

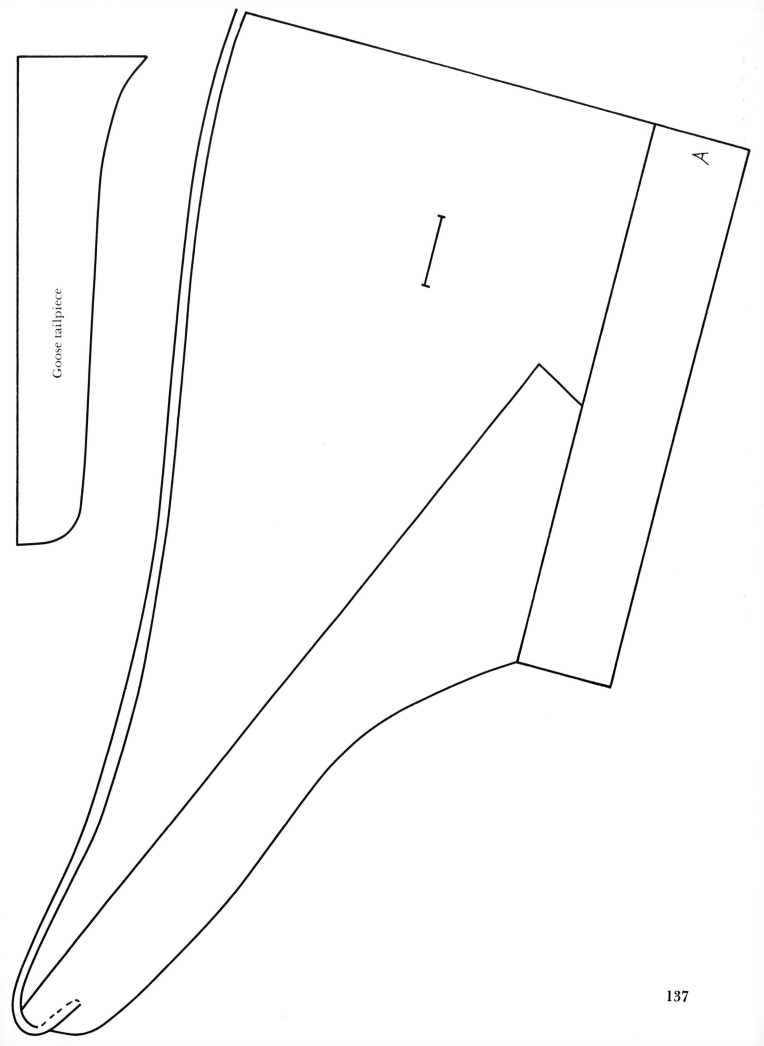

Goose tailpiece

I

A

137

Frank Muller—Currituck Swan and Goose

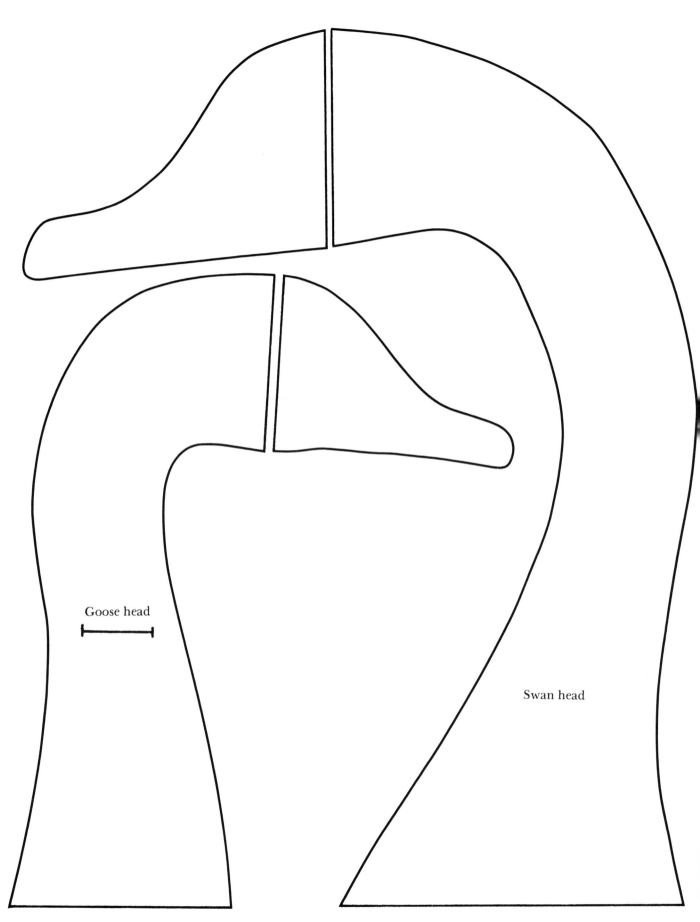

Goose head

Swan head

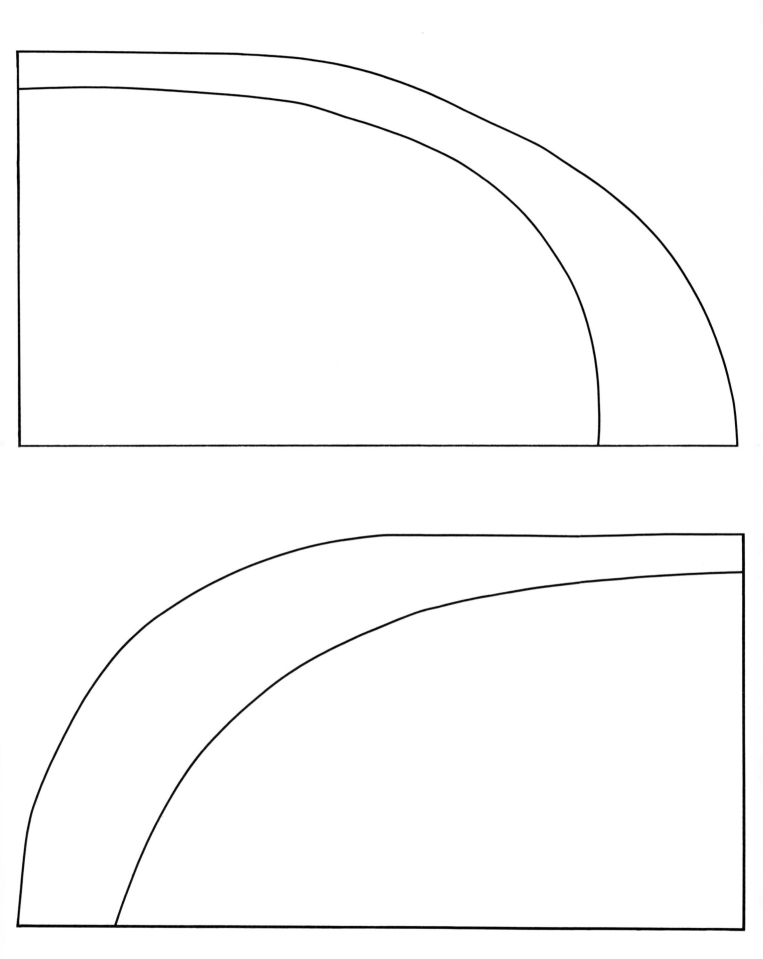

Lay out two-2" x 6" x 22" long boards as shown (18" long for goose).

Use doweling jig and drill stop for 8 dowel holes.

Glue and set dowels in one board.

Dowels in first board. Second board glued and ready for assembly.

Tap boards together.

Clamp and leave set overnight.

Band saw base to shape.

Sand rough edges.

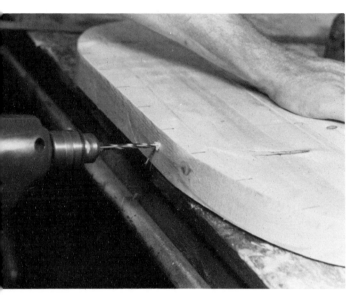

Drill holes for wire except two in front.

Pieces band saw cut for head and neck—note direction of grain.

Use galvanized finish nails and predrill holes for assembly.

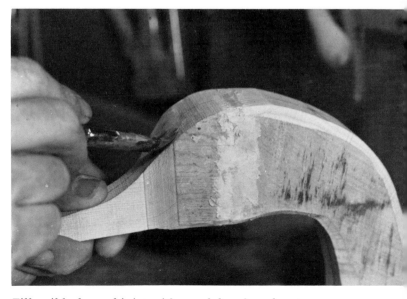

Fill nail holes and joint with wood dough and acetone.

Let sit overnight.

Rough shape on drum sander...

Bill, head and neck.

Final hand sanding.

Center neck on base and predrill for 20D galvanized finish nails—two at front and two at rear.

Glue neck base.

Start nails in predrilled holes.

Finish nailing all four nails.

Center and predrill tail piece.

Glue and nail in place.

Repeat procedure with 6'' high bow support, 5'' high for goose.

Base with head, center support and tail piece in place.

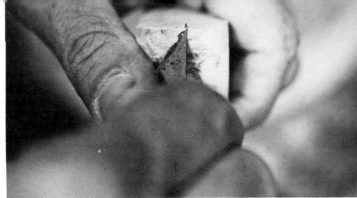

Notch center rear of tail piece for wire bow.

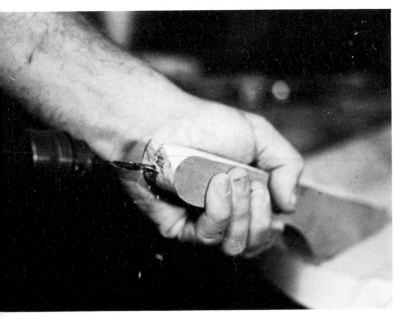

Drill tail, below notch, for wire bow.

Measure 4" from base on back of neck.

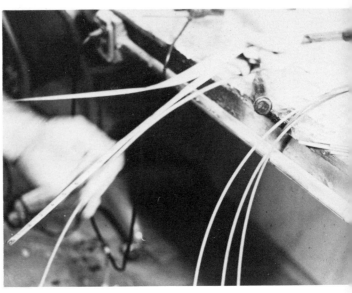

Cut wire bows from 9 gauge or heavier galvanized wire.

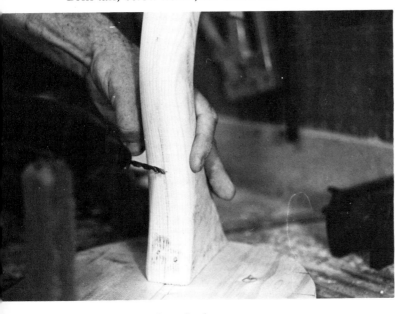

Drill on center for wire bow.

Swan

26"long—center bow	14"—around neck
27"long—tail	23"—center bow
25"—next 4 wires	22"—tail
24"—next wire	21"—5 wires
23"—next wire	19"—next wire
22"—next wire	16"—next wire
20"—next wire	14"—around neck

Cutting wire bows.

Bend ½"—¾" on one end of center bow.

Hook bend in hole in tail piece and push other end into hole in neck.

Shape center bow for desired silhouette shape and tighten by using vise grips and hammer and driving wire into neck.

Secure to center support with galvanized staple.

Add galvanized 4D nail under wire bow (don't drive all way in yet).

145

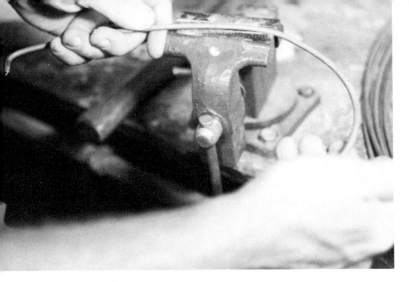

Bend wire for tail as shown.

Mount to base as shown.

Tap wire into predrilled hole.

Should look like this.

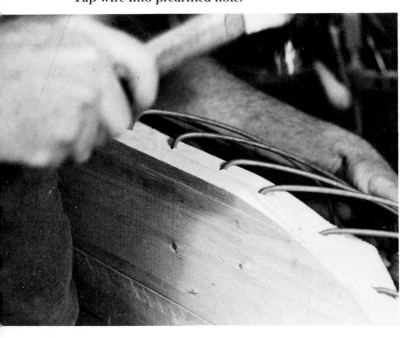

Bend rest of bows and install from tail forward.

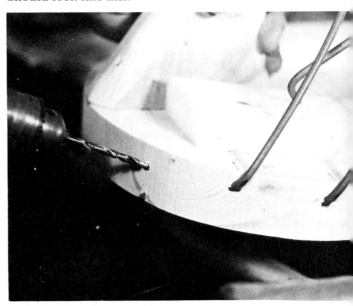

Bend and drill holes for wire around neck. Add two pieces of foam, 2'' wide inside wires and secure with galvanized roofing nails.

146

Flotation and all wires except neck piece in place.

Now install neck piece.

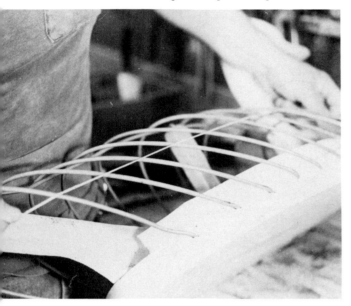

Checking shape with string (all wires should be bent from side to side till all touch string.)

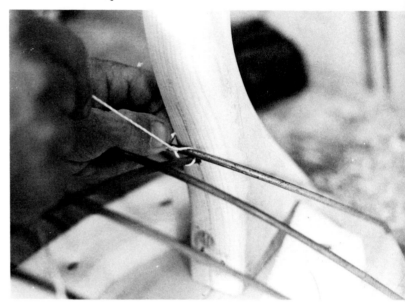

Use nylon string and tie neck piece to center bow.

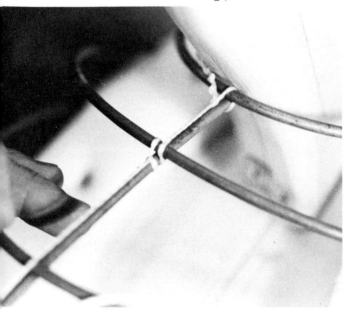

Tie next cross bow to center bow.

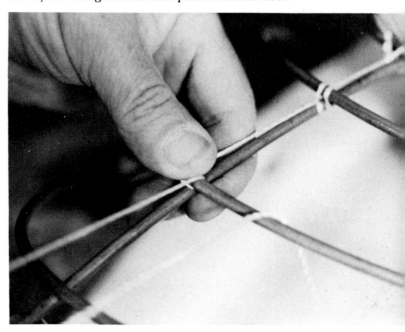

Continue to tail, keeping tight as possible.

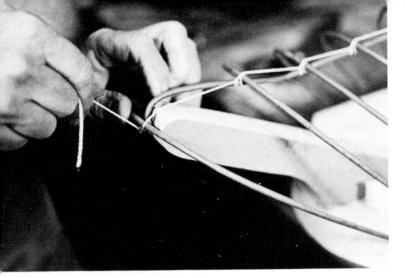

Tie to 4D nail and tap nail in.

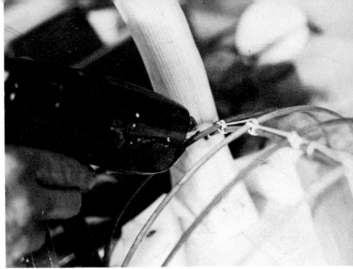

Use waterproof hot glue and glue 1'' strip of canvas over intersection of bows.

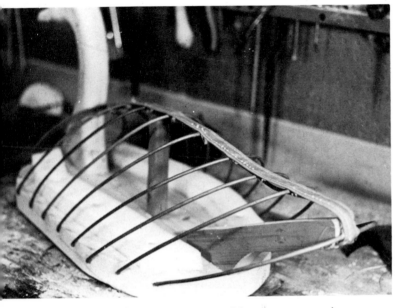

This strip cushions cover and lessens wear on it.

Take 21'' x 34'' piece of canvas, fold lengthwise and secure one end in vise (20'' x 30'' for goose).

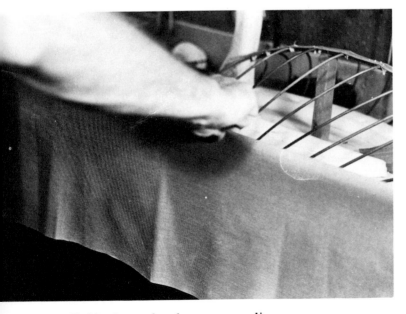

Hold other end and crease centerline.

Mark centerline with chalk.

148

Cut piece out for neck, approximately 1'' wide x 8'' long.

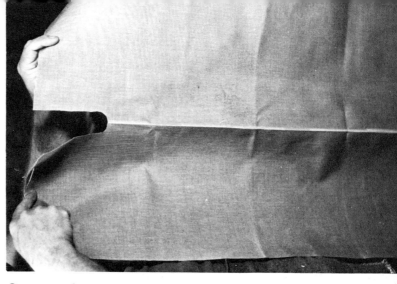

Cut out and centerline shown.

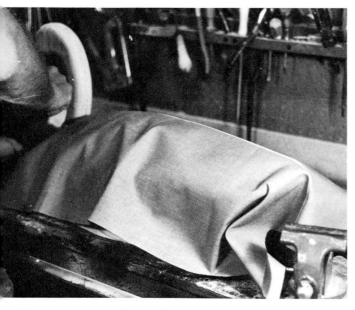

Drape cover over frame.

Position around neck.

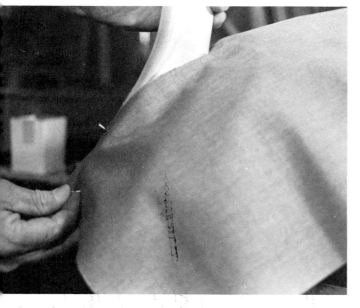

Loosely tack at V in cloth and at base (copper tacks).

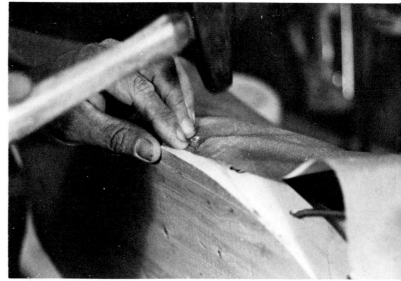

Loosely tack both sides near center, keeping cloth centered on back.

149

Pull and tack cloth under tail piece.

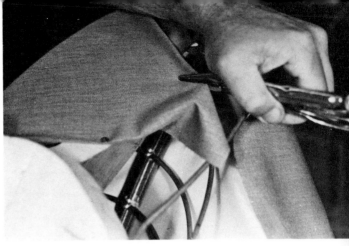

Make fold in cloth, pull tight and tack.

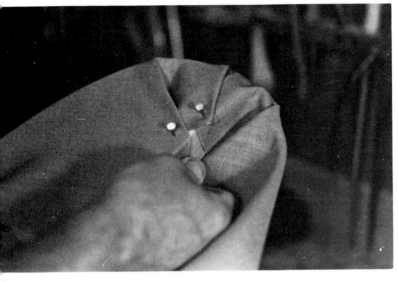

Make second fold and tack.

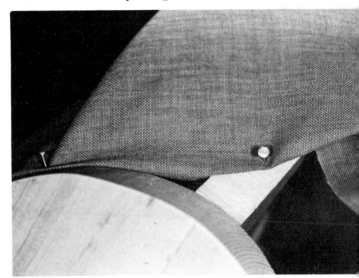

Continue down tail piece, with fold at bottom. Tack near first wire with opening left for self-bailer.

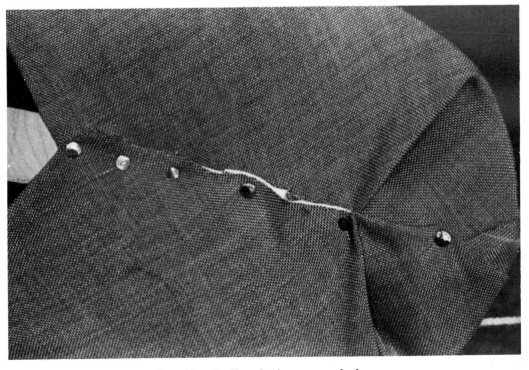

Do other side of tail and trim excess cloth.

150

Continue along one side stretching and tacking cloth in place till neck is reached. Keep center line as close to center of back as possible.

Secure first side and do second side making finish fold at neck.

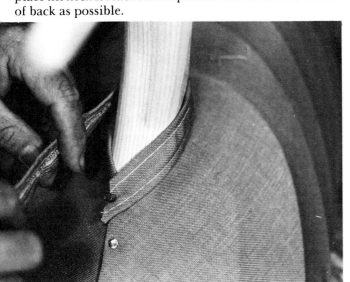

Start finish strip around neck using tack to secure end.

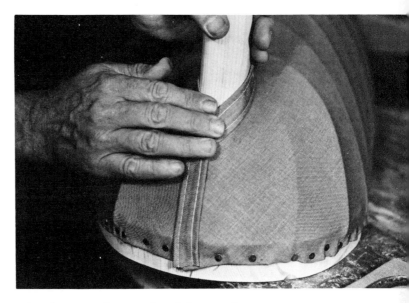

Hot glue or tack around and down to base.

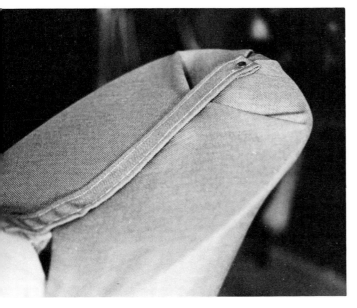

Do same under tail.

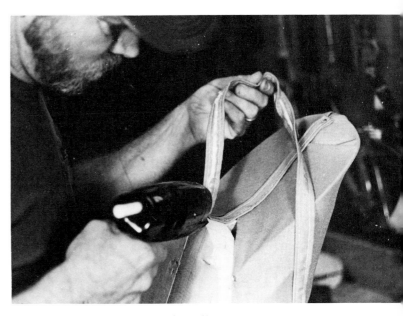

Go around base starting under tail.

151

Strip should cover edge of cover and tacks if possible.

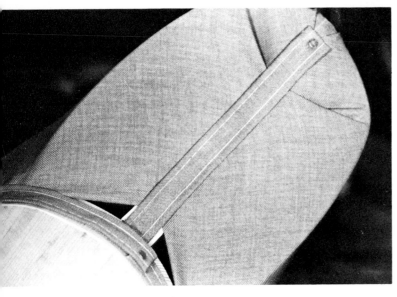

Fold and tack end.

Completed tail section and base strip.

Ralph Nocerino

Black Duck

Ralph, born August 18, 1946, and his wife Carol live in Amity Harbor, New York with their two children, Lori and Dawn. Ralph has been an insurance broker and financial planner for over 20 years. His hobbies include duck hunting, big game hunting, fishing and carving. He has been an avid duck hunter and big game hunter for 30 years. He was introduced to hunting and fishing at the age of six by his grandfather and has been hunting on Long Island's Great South Bay which has been his back yard for 30 years.

His present home is on the waterfront of the Great South Bay, and because of his profession and being self-employed, he has been able to hunt in New York, Canada, Maine and Wyoming.

Being subjected to carving all his life and having seen many of the old baymen of the area carve their own gunning rigs, both for personal use and for sale to other hunters, he began to carve his own personal rig at age 20.

Since most hunting on Long Island Great South Bay is for Black Duck and Broadbill, it was Ralph's intention to make the perfect and most life like Black Duck and Broadbill stool possible.

In 1972 he went to his first decoy show, U.S. National Decoy Show, then in Babylon, New York. At that time he met Al McCormick, who was showing the public how he carved decoy heads and bodies out of cork. He worked with Al for the next two years, helping him make gunning stools at shows and also for sale to friends and others for their own hunting rigs. In the winter of 1974 he carved orders for 22 dozen Black Ducks and Broadbills, which at that time would sell for the cost of wood and cork, which was $120.00 per dozen.

In 1975 Ralph competed in his first carving contest at the U.S. National Decoy Show. Results were: 1st place—Broadbill; 2nd place—Black Duck; 2nd place—Brant. This was the first year that the U.S. National Decoy Show held the gunning stool contest. He also went to the Maryland World Competition. He won 2nd Best in Show—Black Duck.

Since then, he has won over 14 Best in Show, 27 first place, 15 second place, 9 third place ribbons and many honorable mentions.

In 1980 Ralph was asked to be chairman for the U.S. National Decoy Show and he has been serving in this position since then.

At the present time he carves for his personal enjoyment and, at times, takes a few commissions for private collectors.

Ralph gives personal credit and thanks to his wife Carol, who has helped him to paint, and more importantly, to get over losing and go on winning. He also gives credit to Tom, his grandfather who has now passed away, for taking the time to show a young boy the art of hunting and fishing, and for all the stories of years gone by of dogs gunning and decoy carving.

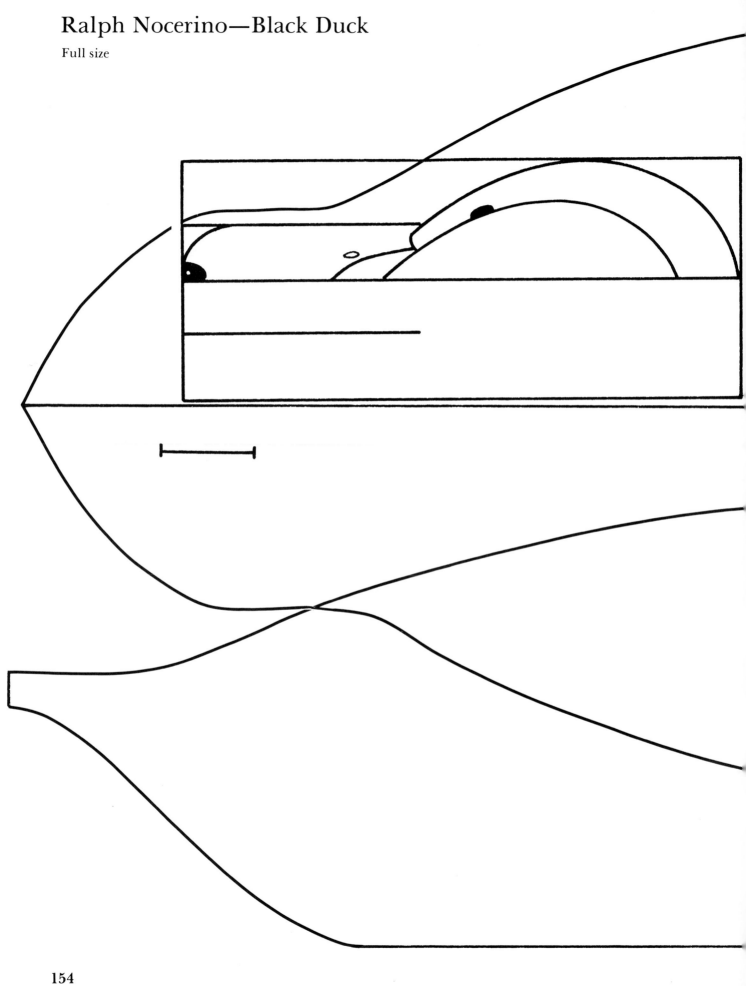

Tracing head pattern on block.

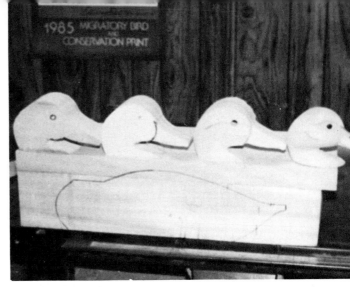

Stages of head from band-sawed blank to finished head.

Body profile traced on block.

Trimming excess wood from head on band saw.

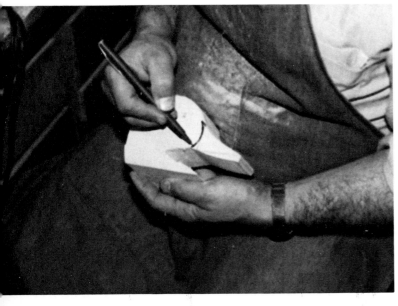

Marking bill on blank.

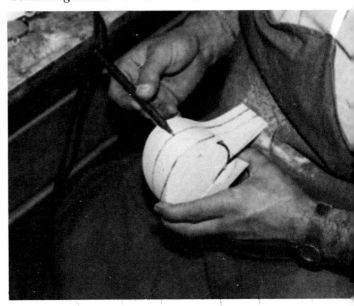

Marking center line on head blank.

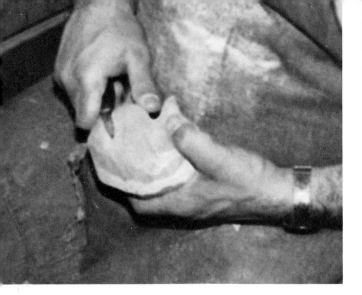

Carving eye channel.

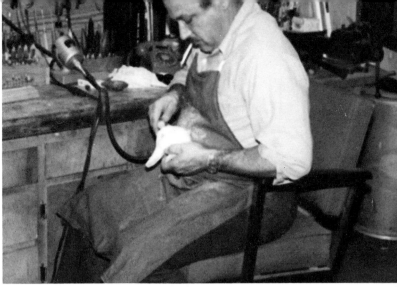

Shaping crown with foredome tool (flexible shaft machine).

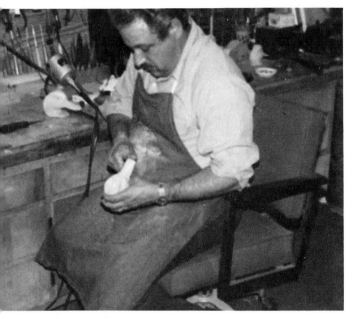

Carving bill with knife.

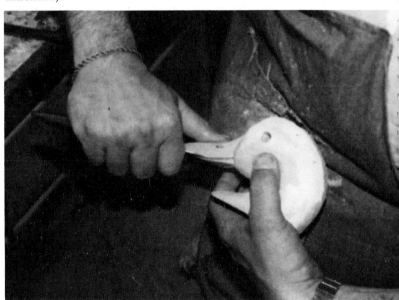

Finishing touches.

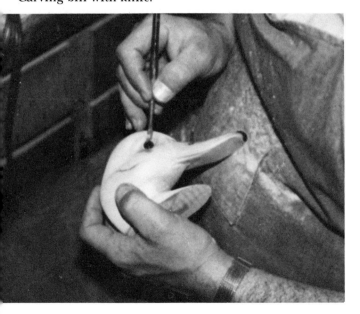

Finishing touches.

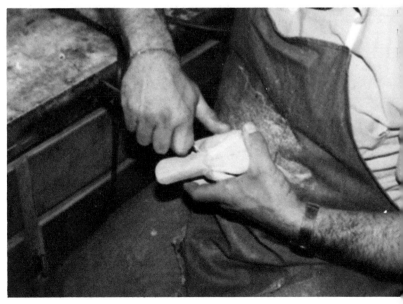

Setting eye and smoothing filler (plastic wood).

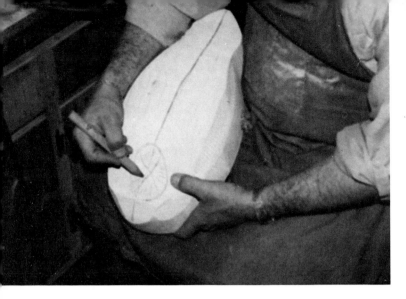

Marking band-sawed body block.

Shaping body with drawknife.

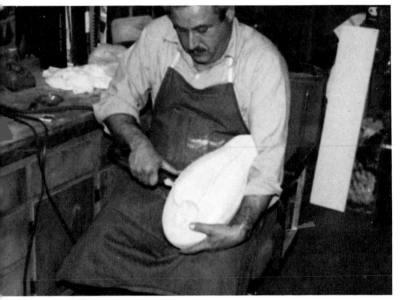

Cutting in side pockets with carbide bit on flexible shaft machine.

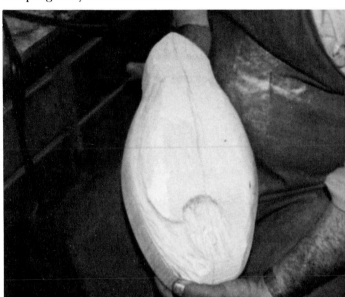

Body block partially shaped.

Squaring off shelf for setting head.

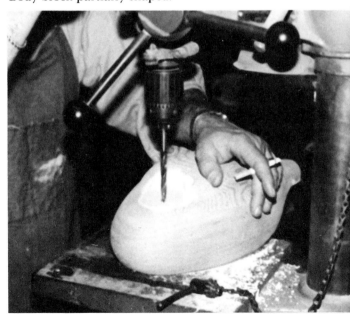

Drilling screw hole.

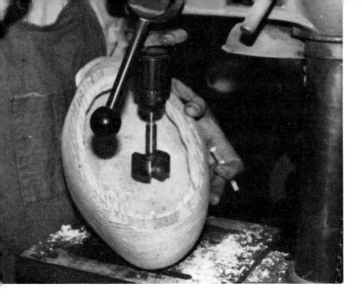

Hollowing with forstner bit.

Cleaning inside with flexible shaft machine.

Drilling screw and epoxy holes in head.

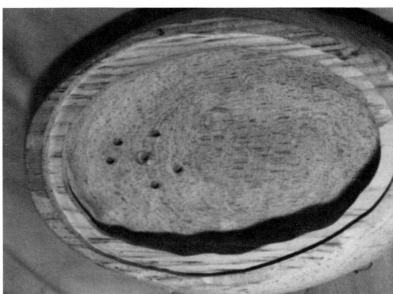

Holes for screw and tuff carve creating cross bond.

Sanding body on drum sander.

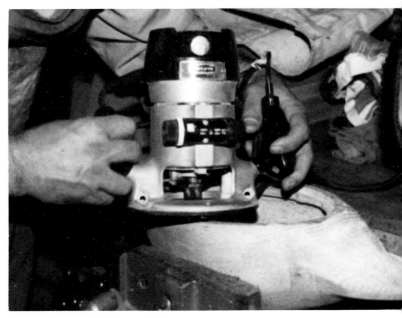

Cutting ledges for bottom plate with router.

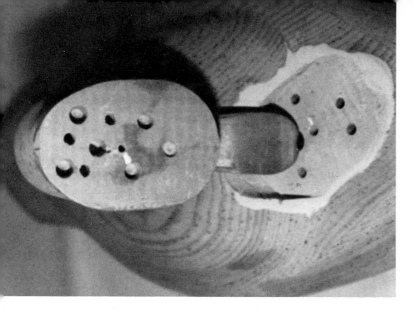

Holes in head and body aligned for heavier gluing.

Setting bottom board with keel.

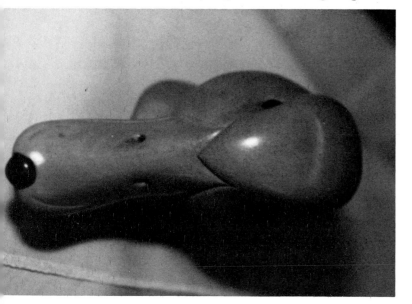

Top view finished bill.

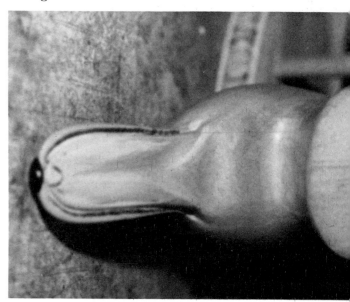

Bottom view finished bill.

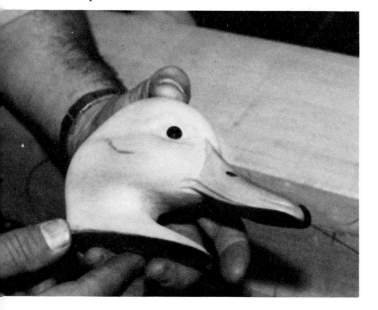

Finished head.

Finished head.

Fitting head to body.

Fitting head to body.

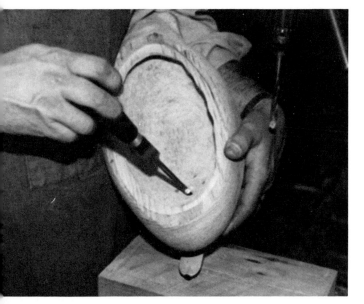

Screwing body to head.

Head set.

Head set, another view.

Decoy sealed and ready to paint.

Roe "Duc-Man" Terry

Whistling Swan

Roe has been carving 17 years, hunting all his life, and guiding hunting parties for ducks, geese and brant for the last five years. Other than his family, gunning is the next most important thing in his life. Roe says, "I live to hunt and love cold winter time. When I returned home from 'Navy boot camp' in 1971, it was December 23rd. I had 15 days leave and was to be married on December 24th. Since I got home late at night on the 23rd, it was too dark to hunt that day, but by 5:30 on the day I was to be hitched, I was sitting in a blind. I got home from gunning at about 10:30 a.m. and by 1:00 p.m. the wedding was in full swing. My lovely bride and I went on a 12 hour honeymoon, only to return on Christmas morning, in time to open presents and go gunning.

I then finished out the rest of my 15 day leave gunning mornings and afternoons, many times, my wife getting up at 4:30 a.m. with me, to take me down to the dock and my boat. We only had one car back then, so if she wanted to use it during the day, she either had to get up and take me or walk down to the dock and get it. I think she realized what she was getting into at that time, and if you don't believe this, just ask her, 'It's a fact.'"

He continued to carve all through his four year Navy service. When he came out of the Navy he went to work as an electronics technician apprentice at the N.O.A.A.C.D.A. station at Wallops Station, Virginia, after working there seven years, he had become a full E.T. but had lost interest in that type of work.

After telling his wife that he wanted to quit his secure civil service job and be a full-time decoy carver and guide, she informed him that if he quit, she was going to divorce him. "I did but she didn't." That was five years ago.

The carvings he does are his own style. He draws all his own patterns and copies no one else's work. He has, however, been influenced by many outstanding carvers such as 'Cigar' Daisey, Dan Brown, Corb Reed and Bobby Umphlett, but mainly by the man who took him under his wing, 'Captain Doug Jester, Jr.', the son of one of the most famous carvers on the east coast. "You see, my dad died when I was nine so 'Captain Doug' taught me how to hunt, fish, clam, carve, drive a boat, etc., etc. Everything you should know about the water and bays between Chincoteague and Wachappague, Virginia, Doug taught me; or at least tried to."

Roe says, " I feel like one of the old timers. If you look back at carving seventeen years ago it'll put you about 1969. Look at some of the old books and winners lists about carving and contests and you'll see that the quality of the decoy was determined by how good the carver was with a hatchet and a knife. Two tools that are used very little, if any, by present day decorative carvers.

Today everything is sculptured, inserted, ground, foredomed or dremeled, everything but 'hand carved'. Maybe I'm just partial to gunning birds, but I'll tell you what; Just where would organizations like the 'Ward Foundation' be if it weren't for people like Lem and Steve, two of the best known *working decoy* carvers that ever lived. The *working decoy* made carving what it is today; a very respected art form."

In the last seventeen years Roe has won about 300 ribbons, trophies and awards for his working decoys and shorebirds, including several 1st, 2nd and 3rd Best of Show awards in both the Working Decoy and Working Shorebird Divisions. He has exhibited and entered contests all around the country and was recently invited to exhibit at the Pacific Flyway Decoy Association Show in Sacramento, California.

"Like I've said, I've been gunning all my life and in those years have helped other guides with their parties. About five years ago I started booking my own parties, and right now, most of the ones I take out have been with me since I started. When I was asked if I thought gunning and duck populations had changed alot since I was a kid, I started feeling old again. On duck and goose hunting in general, I think that overall gunning pressure has driven the birds to harder to get to areas. I don't think there's that many fewer birds, just more hunters.

Like 'Cigar' said the other day when I asked him about gunning and trapping in the *good ole days*. His reply was, 'Hell, this is the good ole days, you're living them right now.' Just think out it, he's right. In the old days you had a flat bottom scow and a shoving pole or an old air cooled outboard of very low horse power. You had to work your tail off to make enough money to buy your gas and oil. In 'Cigar's' day, gunning wasn't a local sport, it was a way of living and making a living. 'You sold your kill or ate it.' Even I can see a big change in gunning from when I was a kid till now.

Mom started letting me hunt alone or with other boys my same age when I was 13 or 14. We worked for our gun shells, gas and oil, and when we came in from gunning we would sell our ducks to buy more shells and go back out again, most of the time we borrowed Elvie Whealton's boat and motor until Jim got his own. Jim Whealton was the first person I can ever remember meeting, I think we were about 4 years old and we've been gunning and fishing together ever since.

When I was in high school, maybe half of the seniors had a car. The parking lot was barely half full each day. Now the high school has three parking lots, solid full of Vets, Trans-Ams and all kinds of fancy cars. Every kid that hunts has a brand new 16' or 18' scow with big outboards. They have all the gas they can burn and all the shells they can shoot. That puts a hell of a lot of pressure on the birds, and it's the same all over the country.

I think too much emphasis is put on limits and habitat. It takes cold weather to drive ducks south. They don't fly down just for a vacation. They move because the cold, ice and snow moves them. You talk about creating habitat in places like Canada and Mexico, why help them? They're shooting the hell out of them in those

places, especially Mexico, where you shoot all you want to. What's needed is to raise more birds in the U.S. like a lot of states have started doing, and like "Ducks Unlimited" is finally doing, with the M.A.R.S.H. program, and quit raising so damn many mallards. They're breeding every true duck out of existance, especially the black duck. I believe a mallard would breed with a goose if the goose would allow it.

The only other comments I've got are these; I realize everyone can't up and quit their job to do what makes them happy, but money ain't everything, I'd rather spend one happy year getting by than 35 years at a job I hate, just hoping to retire some day. 'Son, life is short, maybe I've got a bad attitude, but I say if you've got a dollar, spend it, if you want to do something, do it.'

I'd like to close out with a very special thanks to my wife "Monnie", for her continued support over the years of our marriage, and I mean she's had a lot to put up with. I'd have never made it as a professional carver without her. 'Thanks babe.'"

Roe lives in Chincoteague with his wife, Monnie and their two children, Ryan and Irene. A great thrill for Roe was when his son Ryan won the Jr. Division of the Virginia State Duck Calling Championship.

Roe ''Duc-Man'' Terry—Whistling Swan

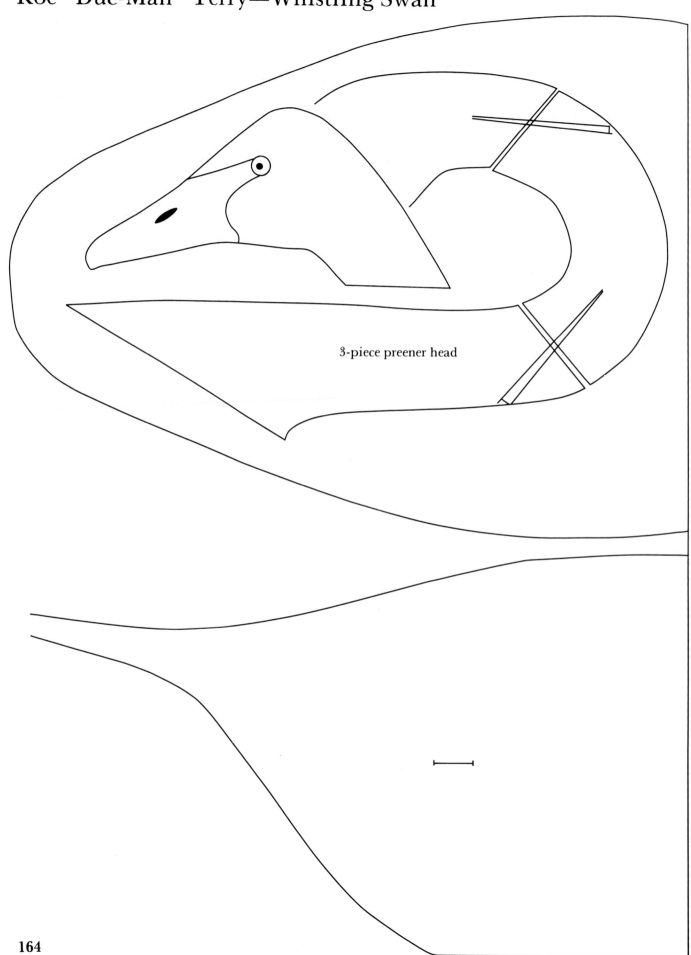

3-piece preener head

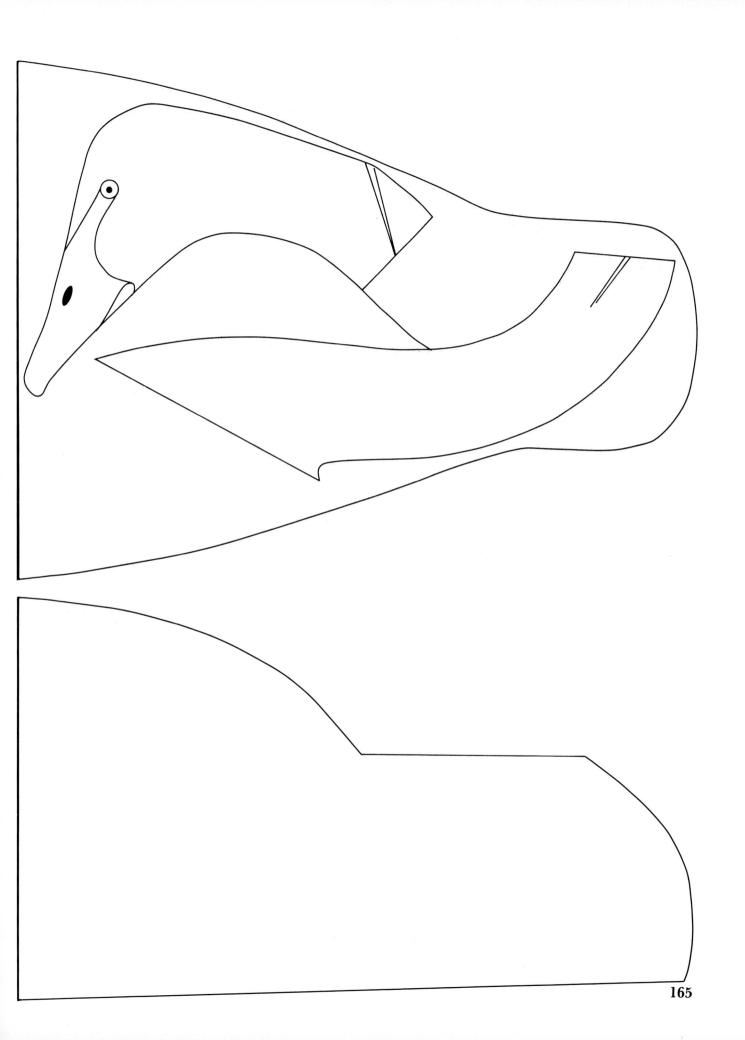

Selection of suitable log.

Squaring log with chain saw.

Marking dimensions of pattern on block.

Marking dimensions of pattern on block.

Marking dimensions of pattern on block.

Block with excess cut away by chain saw.

Block ready for final patterns.

Plan view traced onto block.

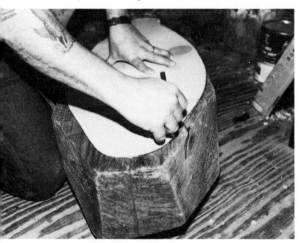

Plan view traced onto block.

Plan view traced onto block.

Profile traced onto block.

Profile traced
onto block.

167

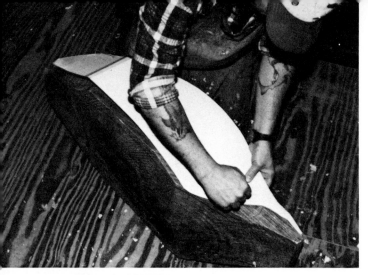 

Tracing profile onto block. Shaping various areas with hatchet.

Shaping various areas with hatchet.

More critical shaping done with large draw knife.

168

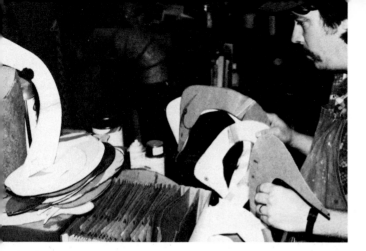

Selection of head pattern.

Tracing profile of head pattern on block.

Tracing profile of neck pattern on block.

Placing head and neck patterns on wood.

Placing head and neck patterns on wood.

Shows joints for twisted neck swan to maintain strength.

Carving neck of swan.

Twisted neck of swan.

170

Carving cheek area.

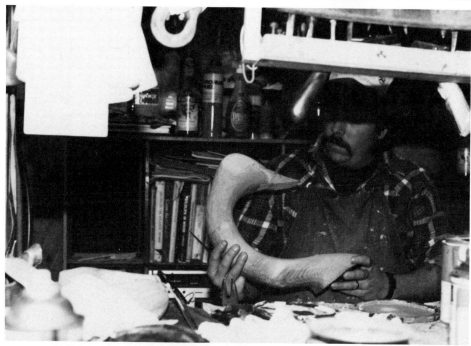
Inspecting the carving.

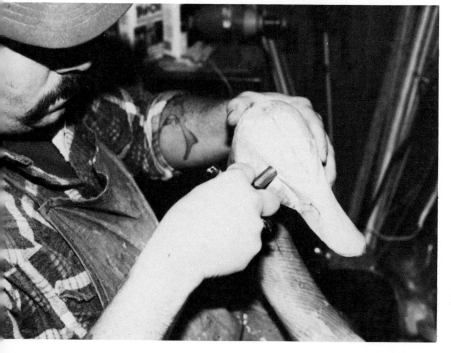
Drilling eye hole.

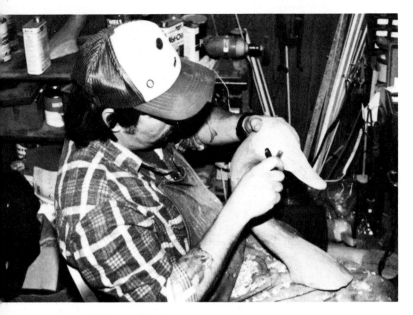

Drilling eye hole.

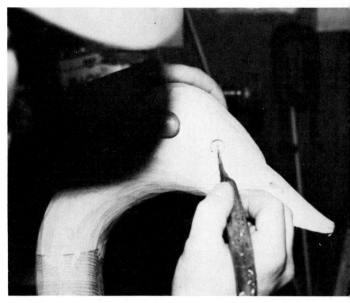

Trimming excess around eye with knife.

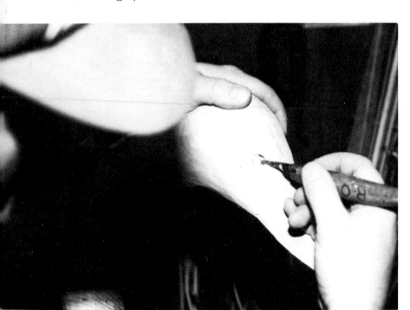

Trimming excess around eye with knife.

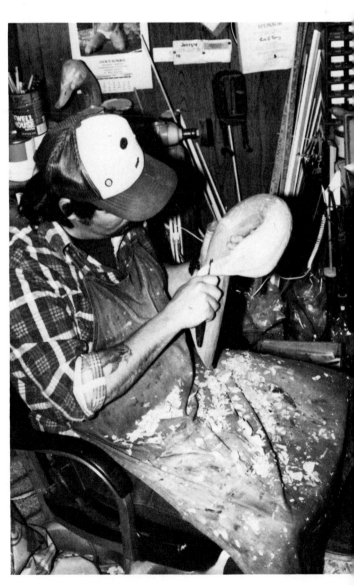

Carving bill.

172

William Veasey

Mallard

Bill Veasey, author of Waterfowl Carving, Blue Ribbon Techniques, is a prolific professional Waterfowl carver and teacher. He has a carving studio and school in Elkton, Maryland where he carves and teaches full time. He has won over 100 awards icluding the head carving trophy at the U.S. National Decoy Contest in New York, two years in a row. Since 1974 his students have captured well over 2500 awards including many "Best in Show" in all classes. Bill's students range in age from 6 years old to 78 years old and most all have won awards in national competition.

Bill is very active in Ducks Unlimited. He is a zone chairman and a national trustee. In 1974 he was made an Honorary citizen of Goldsboro, North Carolina for his help to their fledgling chapter. He donates carvings and runs the auction at many Ducks Unlimited banquets all over the East.

Bill has frequently been guest speaker for various clubs and organizations. He is available to speak on decoys and carvings. He has judged many of the most prestigious shows in the country, and has exhibited extensively throughout the country in all major shows and has had many one man shows. His waterfowl carvings have found their way to 50 states and 8 countries. They are highly detailed in both miniature and lifesize; great effort is exerted to bring lifelike quality to each work. His carvings may be found in private and public collections worldwide.

Bill founded the miniature division of the world class at the Ward Foundation World Championships. He has taught carving at the Philadelphia Museum of Natural Sciences and teaches an accredited course in carving at Clemson University, Clemson, South Carolina, four times a year. In 1981 the Ward Foundation

awarded him their Highest Honor for his overall contribution to the field of waterfowl carving. In 1986 he was elected to the Board of Directors of the Easton Waterfowl Festival, Easton, Maryland.

William Veasey—Mallard

Full size

174

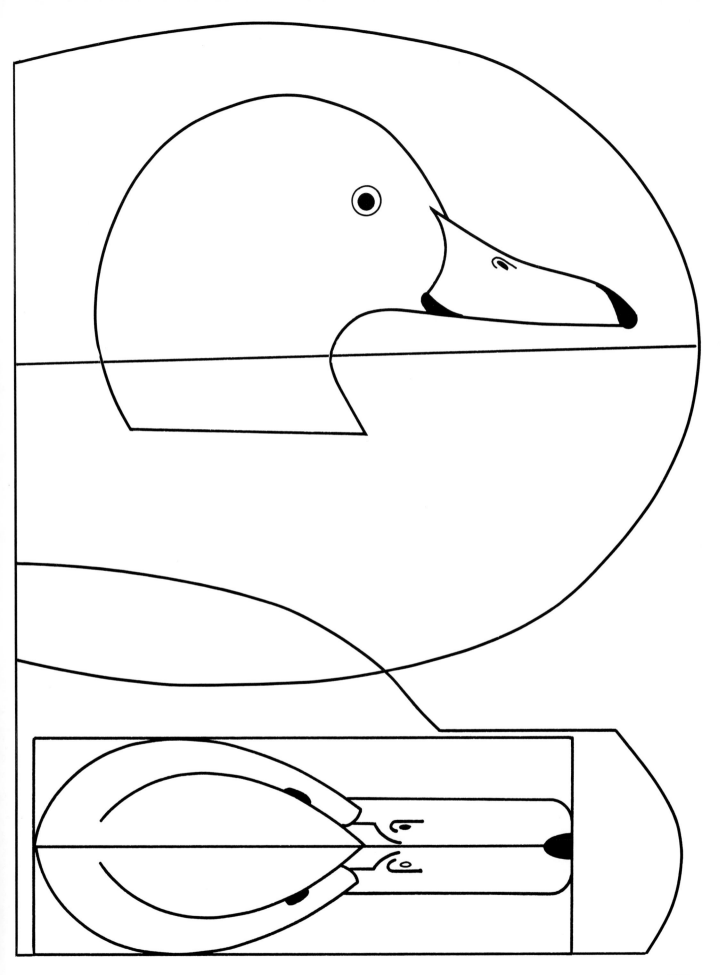

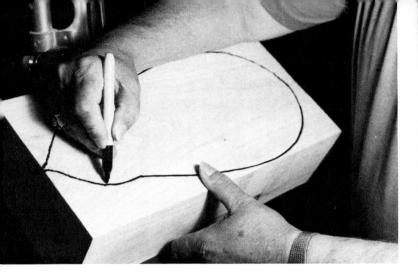

Tracing plan view on block.

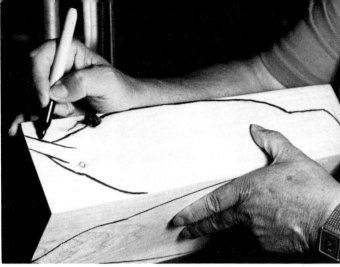

Tracing profile view on block.

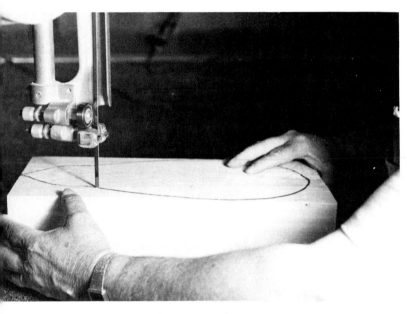

Cutting plan view on band-saw.

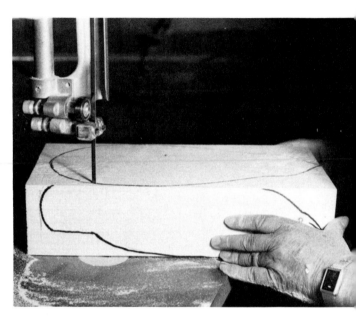

Cutting plan view on band-saw.

Trimming excess wood from band-sawed blank.

Guide marks on bottom.

176

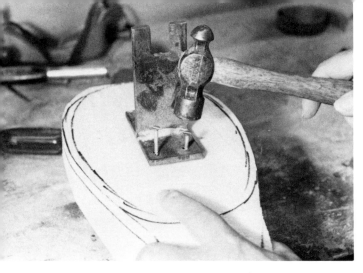

Putting screws in T-Bar on bottom to hold in vise.

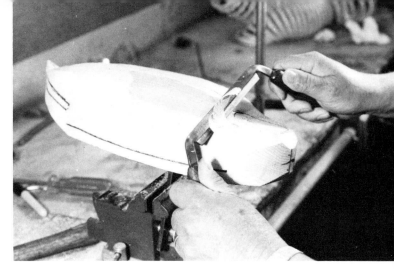

Using draw knife to shape chest area.

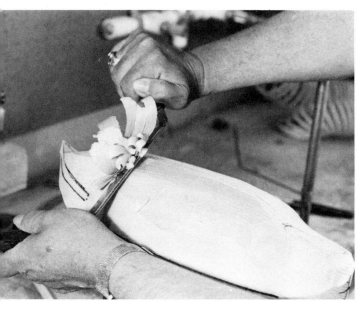

Using draw knife to shape upper rump area.

Using draw knife to shape upper tail area.

Back cut on tail to get shape (note guide lines).

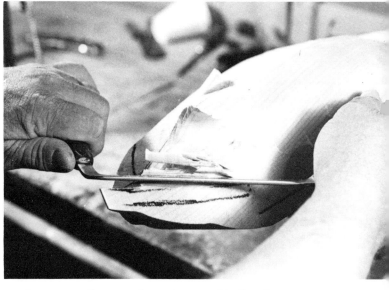

Back cut on tail to get shape (note guide lines).

Shaping under tail with draw knife.

Final shaping under tail with round sur form rasp.

Shaping along bottom with sur form rasp using curved blade.

Final shaping of back and side with sur form rasp.

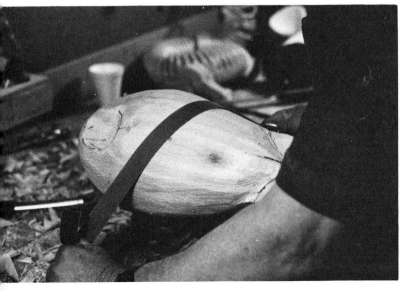

Sanding body with 80 grit strip paper with a shoe shine motion.

Final shaping of tail with knife.

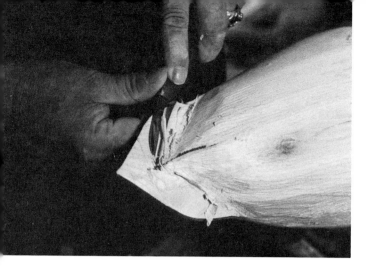

Final shaping of tail with knife.

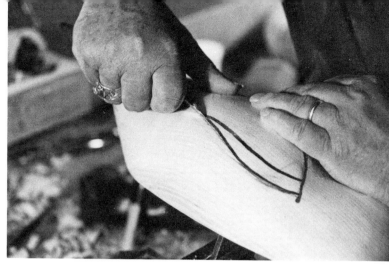

Cutting in of wing area—90° cut.

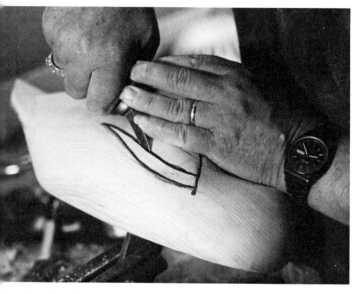

Cutting in of wing area—90° cut.

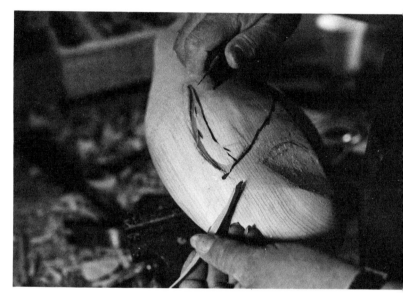

Slice cut out.

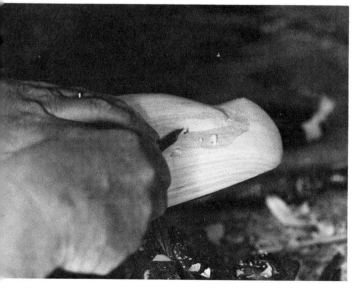

Flowing cut away from intersection fanning wing and side pockets.

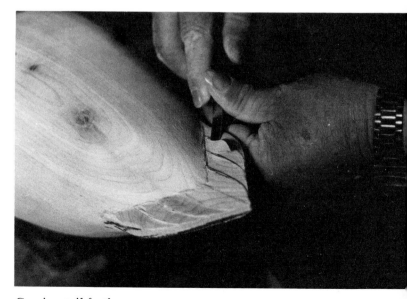

Carving tail feathers.

Layout of primaries, secondaries, tertials and tertial coverts.

Carving of primaries, secondaries, tertials and tertial coverts, etc.

Tracing bottom of decoy onto bottom board (⅛ wood paneling).

Inner line to be cut out for bottom insert.

Insert cut out on band-saw.

Setting nails in bottom board template.

180

Trace bottom board onto decoy.

Nail template onto decoy.

Use router to cut ledge for bottom board to set in bottom of decoy—a lettering guide is used to ride on template.

Remove template.

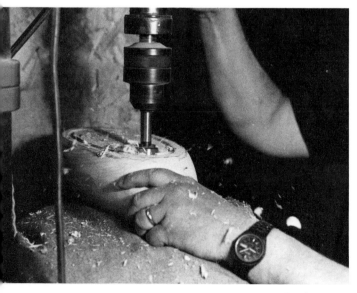

Drill into interior making sure to leave ledge for bottom board.

Further hollowing with forstner bit.

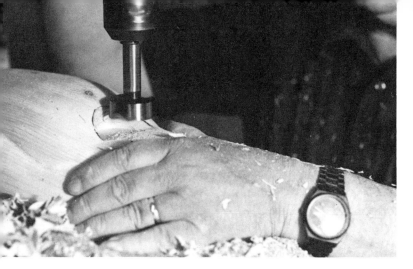

Cutting head shelf with 2'' forstner bit.

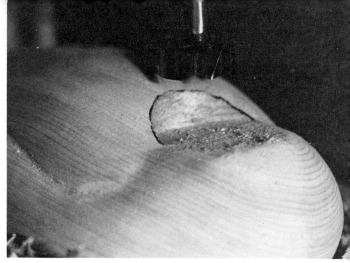

Cutting head shelf with 2'' forstner bit.

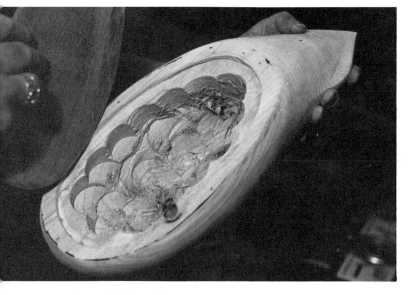

Decoy hollowed.

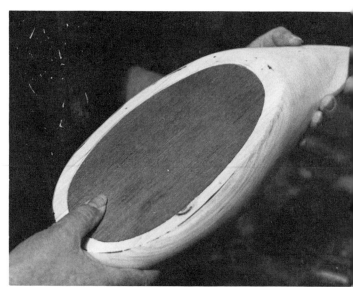

Bottom plate fitted.

Gluing in bottom plate using 5-minute epoxy.

Drilling holes in keel for lead to be poured for ballast.

Drill out small knots.

Fill knot holes with plastic wood.

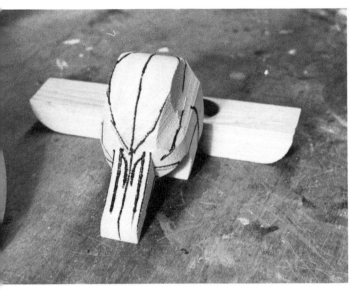

Roughed out head with guide marks.

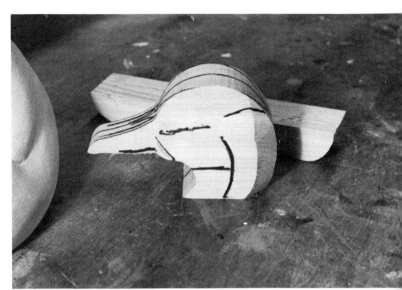

Roughed out head with guide marks.

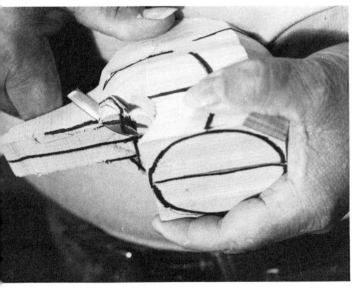

First cut, back cut along bill.

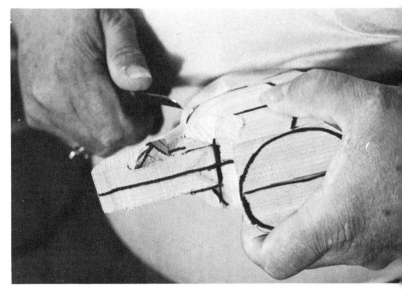

90° cut to this so as to define bill full length or underside (this will vary according to pattern and position of bill).

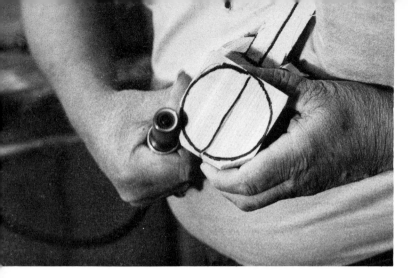

Shaping back of head with foredom or flexible shaft machine.

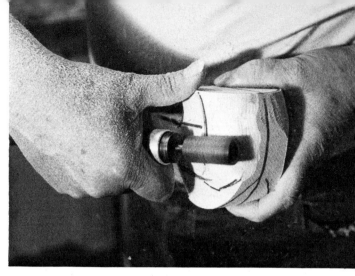

Shaping back of head with foredom or flexible shaft machine.

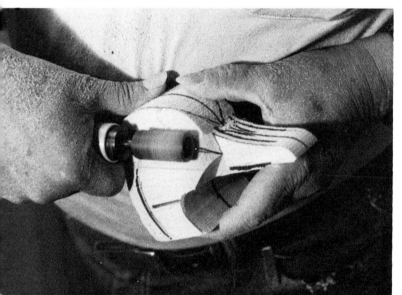

Carving eye channel—note position of bit.

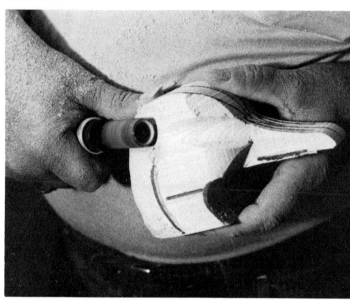

Flowing eye channel into back of crown.

Shaping back of cheek area.

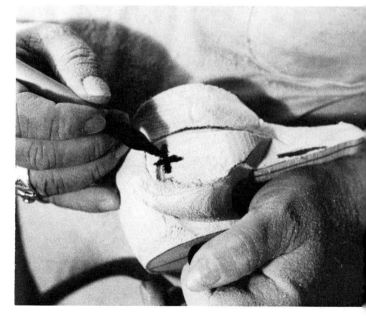

Marking high point of cheek.

184

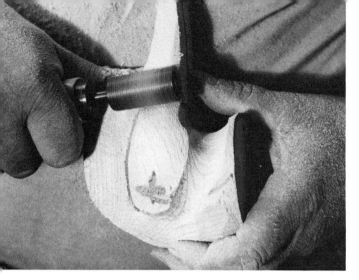

Sloping from high point to bill in an arc or egg shape.

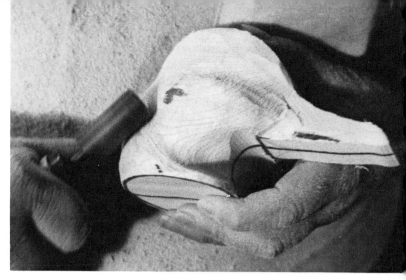

Flowing lines together.

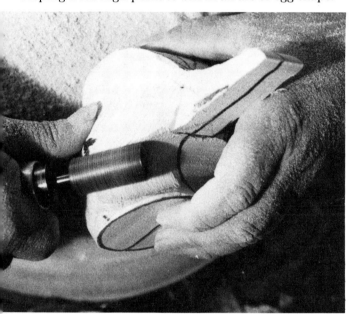

Cutting under cheek to form throat and cheek lines.

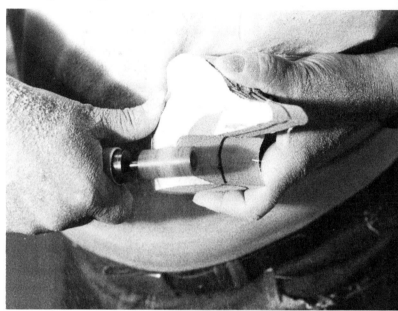

Cutting under cheek to form throat and cheek lines.

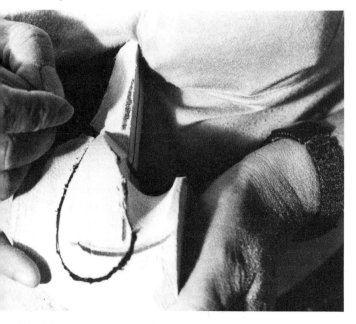

Marking egg shape of cheek.

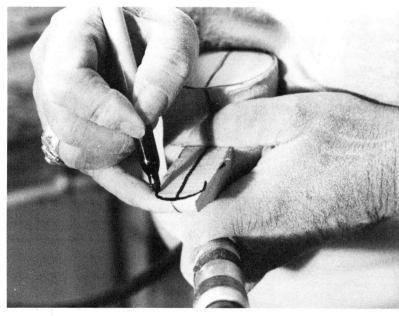

Marking end of bill.

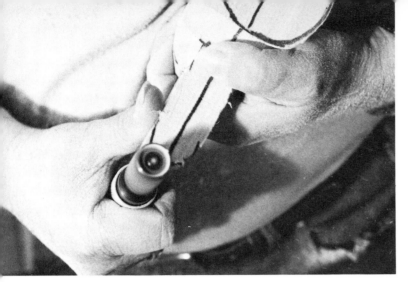

Shaping end of bill.

Back cut along upper bill line into forecrown.

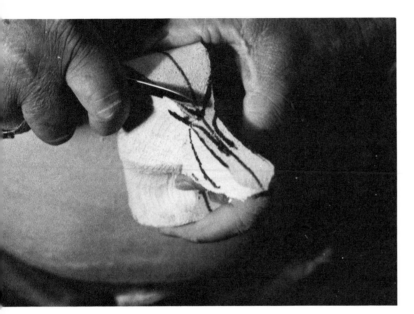

90° cut to this.

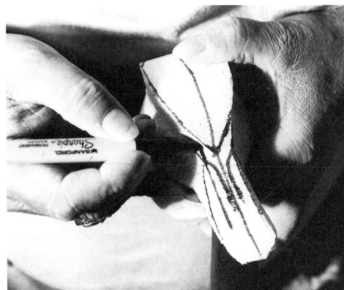

Extend pencil line to crown, forming shape of culmen.

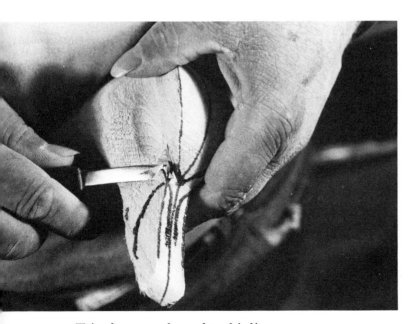

Trim from eye channel to this line.

Cut across angle of upper bill.

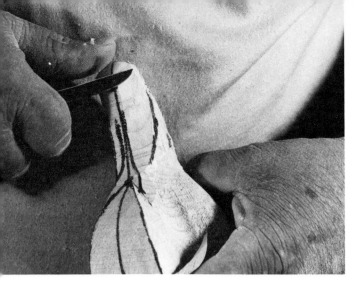

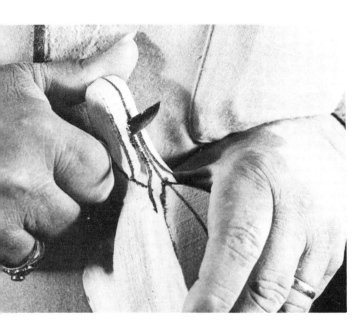
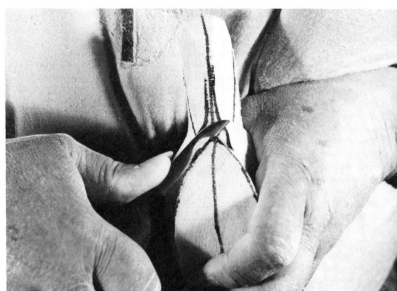

Shaping other side of bill, same as previous steps.

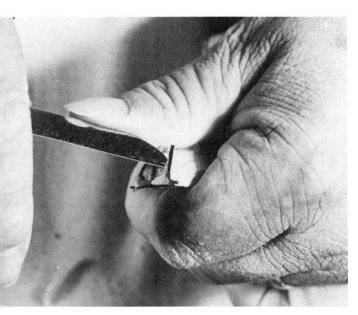
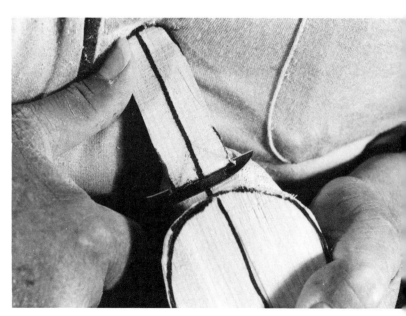

Carving the nail.

Cutting in under bill.

187

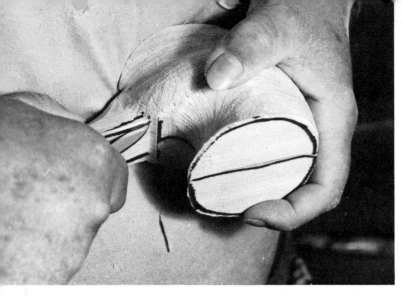
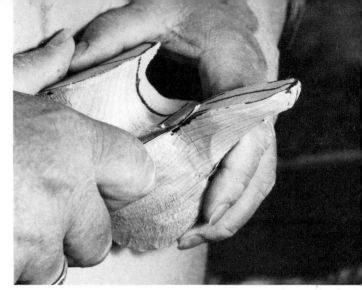

Carving separation under bill.

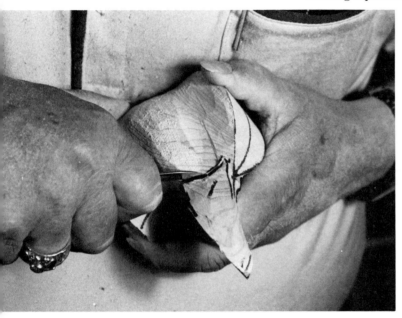

Carving separation between head and bill.

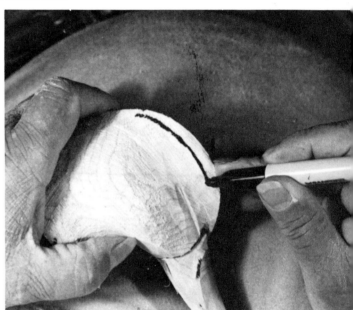

Marking crown roll over.

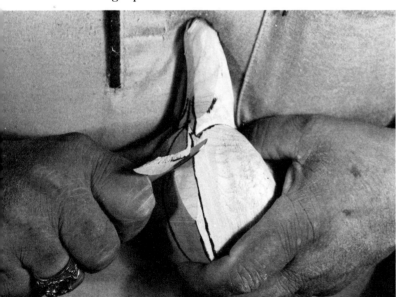

Carving crown.

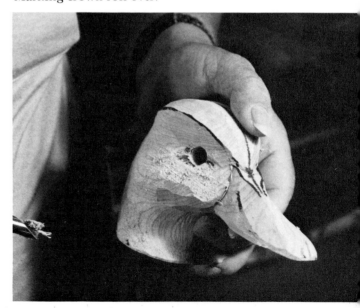

Drilling 10mm eye for brown eye.

188

Sanding under bill with "tootsie roll" or cartridge sander.

Using burner to refine nostrils.

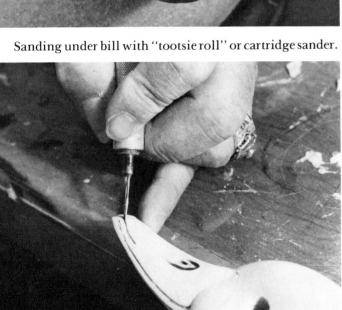

Using burner to refine bill indentations.

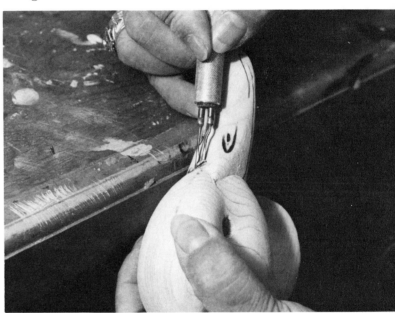

Using burner to refine culmen.

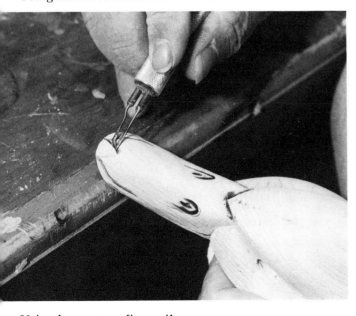

Using burner to refine nail.

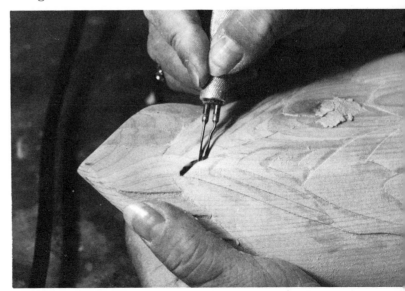

Using burner to outline carved feather groups (quicker and easier than sanding).

Mixing 5-minute epoxy to set head.

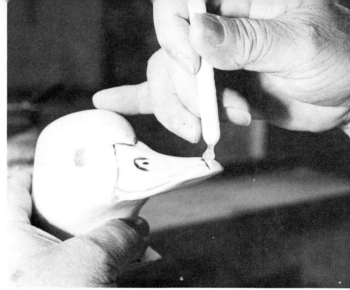

Using 5-minute epoxy to reinforce nail for strength.

Head set.

Flowing head to body.

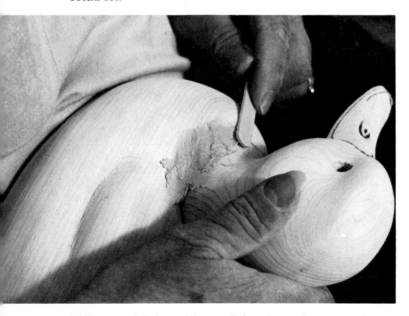

Filling neck joint with wood dough or plastic wood.

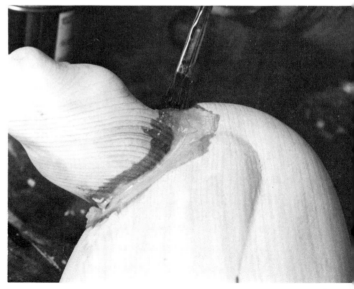

Use large amount of acetone to smooth wood dough. This eliminates a great deal of sanding.

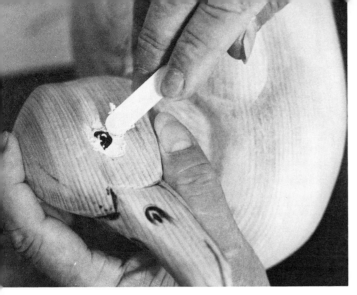

Use moldable epoxy to set eye and small build up around eye.

Dampen finger and smooth epoxy into wood.

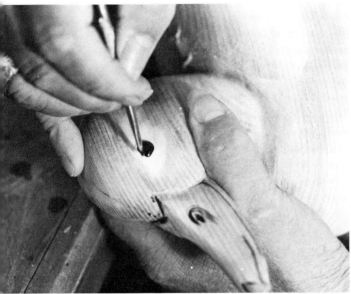

Shape eye lid area with small paint brush using water.

Seal with shellac or deft using Krylon gray to undercoat middle of decoy (ready to paint).

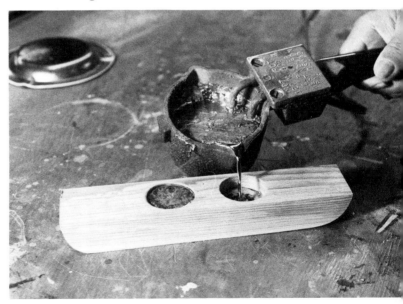

Pouring ballast into keel.

Gilmore "Butch" Waggoner

Upper Bay Canvasback

In 1947, Gilmore "Butch Wagoner was born in Havre de Grace, Maryland, a city which is considered the "Decoy Capital of the World." As Butch grew up in this historic town on the shore of the Chesapeake Bay, he naturally acquired an early interest in the hunting activities for which the area is so famous. Butch was hunting rabbits and squirrels when he was 9 years old; and by age 13, he was hunting waterfowl. He couldn't afford to buy decoys, so he and his friends made their own, first by painting old milk jugs, and then by advancing to making crude wood decoys with a hatchet.

This growing interest in decoy-making was of course stimulated by the legacy of the early decoy makers of Havre de Grace—crafstmen such as Sam Barnes, Jim Currier, the Hollys, Bob McGaw, and Charles Barnard. Present-day inspiration in Havre de Grace is Madison Mitchell.

Butch found a deep-seated interest in working with wood and making decoys. At age 20 he started working part-time with Jim Pierce. Later he decided to ask the master decoy maker Madison Mitchell for a part-time job. He didn't wish to be paid in dollars but in decoys; and Butch now has many fine Mitchell decoys in his collection as a result of his apprenticeship in the Mitchell shop. Butch worked up the Mitchell apprentice scale first in the pole yard splitting decoy blanks, next assembling and nailing heads, then to the bandsaw shed where he roughed out decoy body blocks and heads. He then advanced to running the duplicating machine and then to the prime and putty stage. Through his five years with Madison, Butch learned well the techniques of the master.

In 1979 Butch decided to start on his own, and during the first year he traded his labor to Paul Gibson in return for the use of his duplicating machine. In 1980 Butch built his own duplicating machine and his own decoy shop. At times he has some young helpers assist at the shop, but generally he works alone save for the help of his wife, Ann.

The Wagoner decoy has a cedar body (which usually is the final stop for a piece of an old utility pole). The body is formed on a duplicating machine and then finished by draw knife and sanding. The heads are usually basswood carved by a small draw knife and a regular knife. The heads are fastened to the body with glue, dowels and nails. After sanding and priming it's impossible to tell where the glue line was. Butch uses rustoleum oil paint as well as artist's oils. He usually has two primer coats and at least one finish coat. There can be as many as five coats on some birds such as the pintail. All his decoys are sold with the home-cast lead keel weight and brass tie ring and staple.

Butch's decoys are hard to discern from those made by Madison Mitchell. To avoid any confusion, Butch always signs his birds on the bottom. He also changes just enough of the primary feathering so that a knowledgeable person can tell the difference. Butch's wife, Ann, calls her husband's work "the affordable Mitchell decoy."

Butch makes and sells around 400 decoys per year. He makes all species of ducks as well as geese and swan. He rarely has extras on hand, and if you want one of his decoys, you have to get on the waiting list. Butch presently has about 300 decoys back ordered. His customers come from everywhere.

A number of people still order from Butch with the intent of using the decoys for gunning, and Butch always tries to accommodate the hunters.

With decoy makers like Butch in the Havre de Grace area, the legacy of the old decoy makers will continue.

GILMORE "BUTCH" WAGONER

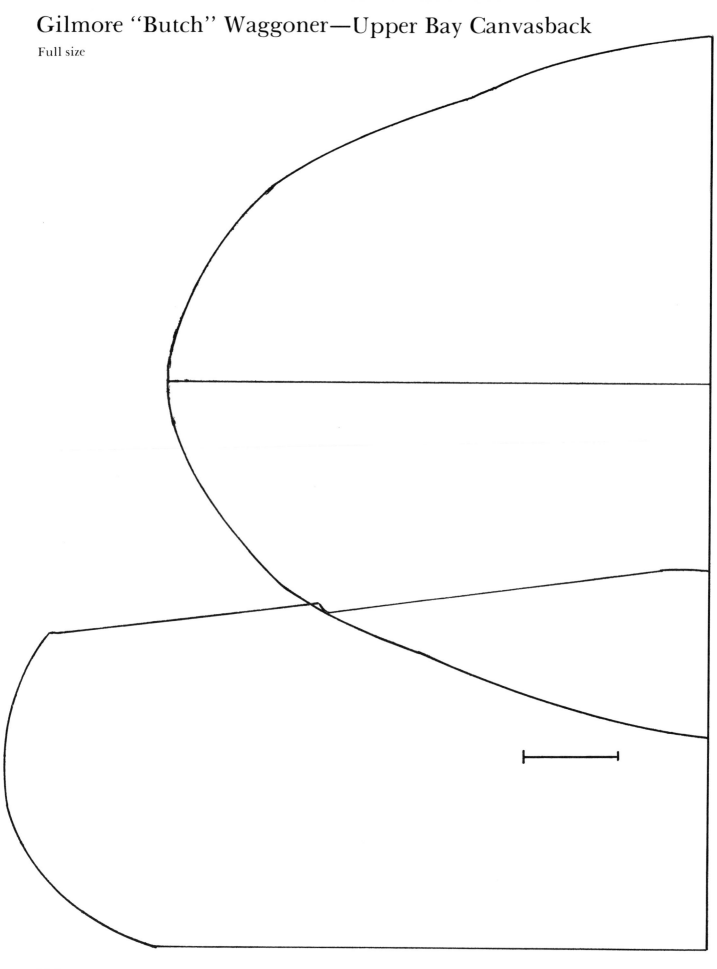

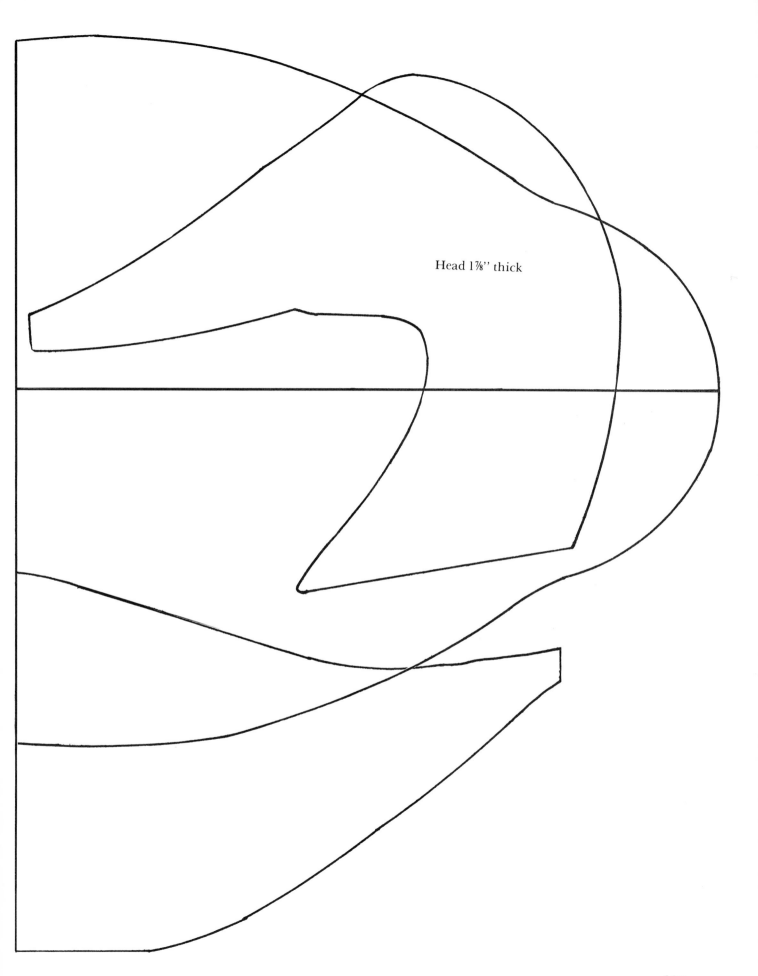

Head 1⅞'' thick

Log pile (white cedar telephone pole.)

Measuring log for canvasback bodies.

Measuring log for canvasback bodies.

Cutting blocks with chainsaw.

Centering log for splitting.

Splitting blocks.

196

Marking pattern on block.

45° cut off of excess wood.

Havre de Grace "special" carving machine made by "Butch" patterned after World War I type gunstock machine.

Fitting block to machine.

197

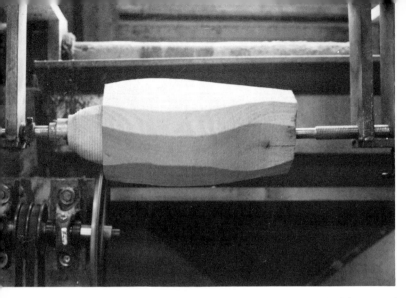
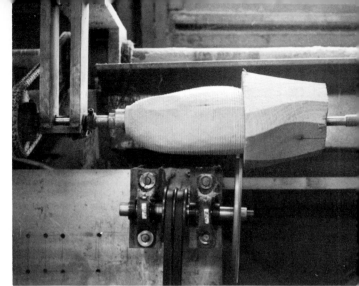

Machine turning body block.

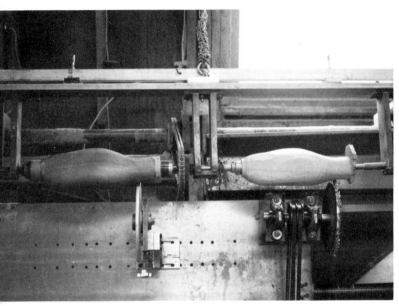

End of pattern or master.

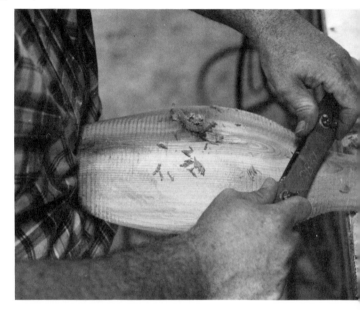

Spokeshaving turned block.

Spokeshaving turned block.

Further spokeshaving.

Spokeshaving body.

Trimming machine end off breast on band saw.

Trimming machine end off tail on band saw.

Shaping tail with drawknife.

Shaping under tail with drawknife.

Shaping breast with sur form rasp (flat blade).

Shaping tail with sur form rasp.

Further shaping with sur form rasp.

Sanding body with 6'' pneumatic drum sander.

Layout of head pattern 1 7/8'' stock—bill in line with grain of wood for maximum strength.

200

Band-sawing head pattern.

Center lining band-sawed head.

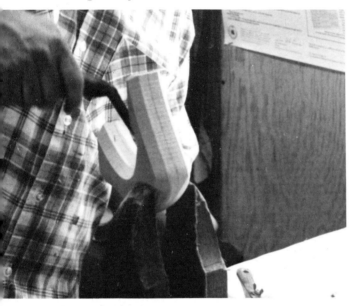

Shaping head with drawknife.

Shaping bill with drawknife.

Spokeshaving back of head.

Spokeshaving back of head.

Shaping under throat using die grinder with carbide bit.

Shaping head with knife.

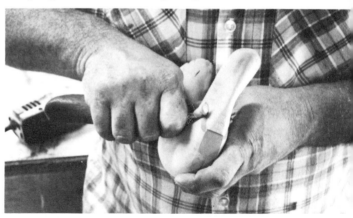

Cutting in the "gills".

(Author's note: All carvers know that ducks do not have gills, however somewhere in history someone in the Havre de Grace area started calling the cutting in of the bill simply "cutting in the gills". To this day all Havre de Grace carvers refer to this step in this way and teach the new decoy makers to do the same. It is a long standing habit that will probably persist for a long time).

202

Cutting in the bill.

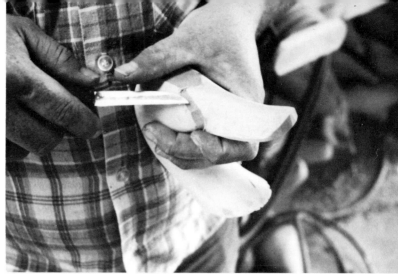

Cutting in the gills.

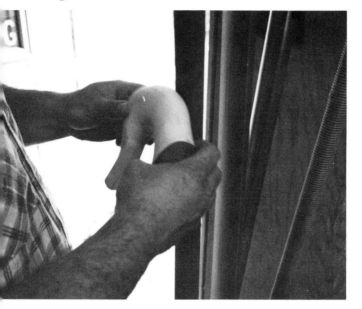

Sanding head on belt sander.

Drilling pilot holes for head nails (30 penny).

Setting head with epoxy and 30 penny nail (in front two 2½'' staples are used to firmly anchor head.

Head set and ready to sand finished decoy.

Harry J. Waite
Bufflehead

In 1958 H.J. Waite was one of the few full time carvers in the U.S. At the ripe age of 21 his carvings were featured in Abercrombie and Fitch's prestigious Fifth Avenue window. This began an instant demand for his distinctive work. One of the first to feature birds in flight, Harry's work is recognized for its wood grained feathering and stylized heads. This carver has an uncanny ability to capture the attitude and personality of the bird.

Much of Harry's work has been "functional" art. Doors, chests, tables, cupboards and cabinets have been graced with his renditions of swaying cattails and flying birds.

His life has been spent totally involved with the outdoors. Hunting, fishing, and a "Pied Piper" personality have enabled him to develop his talent to its high standards of today. These carvings can be found in collections throughout the world.

Today, as in 1958, Harry can be found in his renovated 1721 grist mill. Here he happily lives and carves with his charming wife and two lively sons.

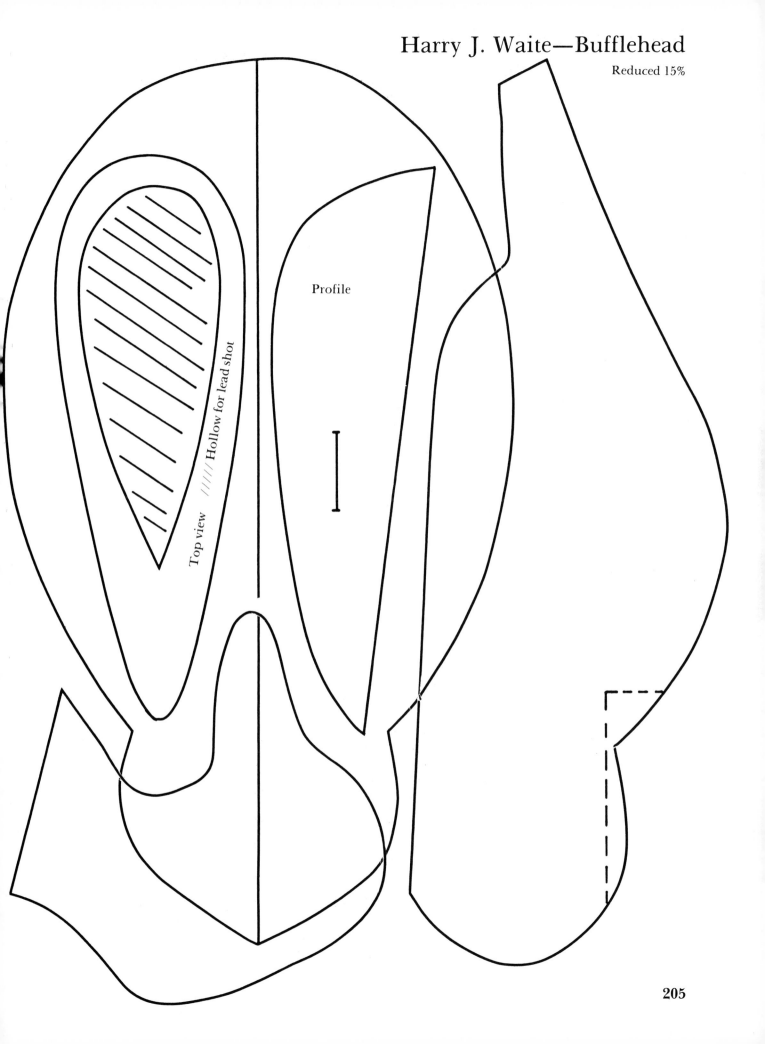

Harry J. Waite—Bufflehead

Reduced 15%

Top view ///// Hollow for lead shot

Profile

The master at work—carving a head out of sugar pine.

The head partially carved (note open bill-cut with bandsaw).

Profile of head with bill cut in to separate head.

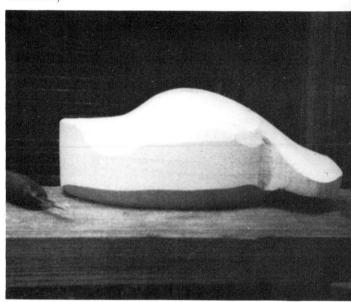

Band sawed body block profile.

Band sawed body block, top view with guide lines.

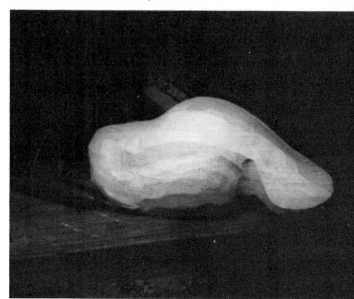

Body block partially shaped.

206

Body shaped and tail feathers carved in.

Body cut along predetermined line and hollowed for better floatability.

Fitting head to body.

Finished carving of decoy.

Torching decoy to raise grain. (This is a H.J. Waite trademark)

207

Gallery of Finished Decoys

Coot Drake

Red Squaw Drake

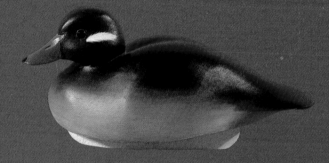

Bufflehead Hen

Blue-Winged Teal Drake

Brant Drake

Goldeneye Drake

Canvasback Drake

Snow Goose Drake

Carved by William Veasey. Courtesy of the James Dodd Collection.

Carl Addison—Ring-Necked Duck Drake

Robert Biddle—Baldpate Drake

Dan Brown—Green-Winged Teal Drake

Dan Brown—Green-Winged Teal Hen

Paul Dobrowski—Canvasback Hen

Delbert "Cigar" Daisey—Atlantic Brant

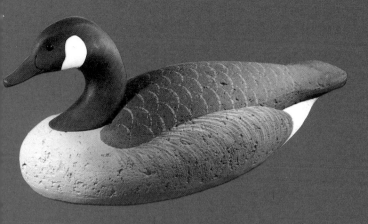

Harold Haman—Canada Goose

Charlie "Speed" Joiner—Wood Duck Drake

Charlie "Speed" Joiner—Wood Duck Hen

Ned Mayne—Red Head Drake

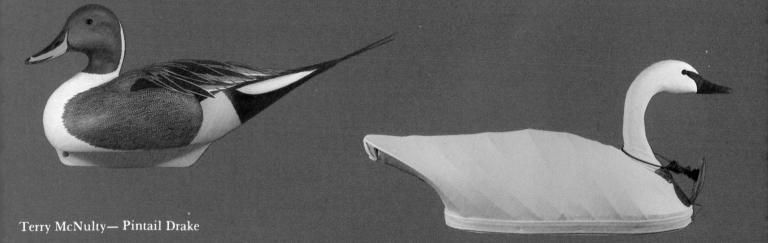

Terry McNulty— Pintail Drake

Frank Muller—Currituck Swan

Frank Muller—Currituck Goose

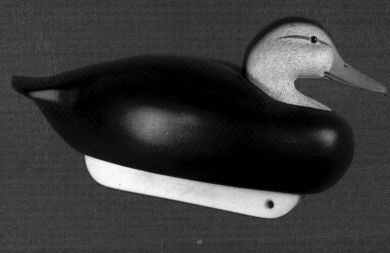

Ralph Nocerino—Black Duck

Roe "Duc-Man" Terry—Whistling Swan

William Veasey—Mallard Drake

Gilmore "Butch" Waggoner—Upper Bay Canvasback

Harry T. Waite—Bufflehead Drake

Carl Addison—Ring-Necked Duck Drake

Under tail feathers

Black umber 2
Raw umber 2
Iridescent white 1
Mars black 1
equals

Upper tail feathers

Burnt umber 2
Raw umber 2
Titanium white 1
Mars black 1
equals

Under tail feathers (edges)

Burnt umber 2
Raw umber 2
equals

Upper tail feathers (edges)

Unbleached titanium white 3
Raw umber 1
equals

Chest and rump feather

Mars black 2
Burnt umber 1
Raw umber 1
equals

Chest and rump feather (edges)

Mars black 3
Alizarin crimson 1
equals

Outer (2nd layer) Chest and rump feather (edges)

Mars black 10
Unbleached titanium white 1
equals

Outer Chest and rump feather (edges)

Mars black 5
Unbleached titanium white 1
equals

Secondaries

2   Raw umber

1   Unbleached titanium white

1   Mars black

equals

Back and primary feathers and tertials

1   Sap green

1   Alizarin crimson

equals

Head

3   Dioxazine purple

Mars black

1

equals

Secondaries (edging)

Titanium white, rear edge

Mars black, forward edge

Crown of head and back of neck

Ivory black

Bill—Trim out in titanium white and ivory black.

Paynes gray

3

Titanium white

1

equals

Sides

1   Burnt umber

1   Raw umber

2   Titanium white

equals

5   Unbleached titanium

Sides—Wash and then feather with titanium white

Wash back and primaries with mars black.

Top view of finished decoy.

Bottom view of rump area.

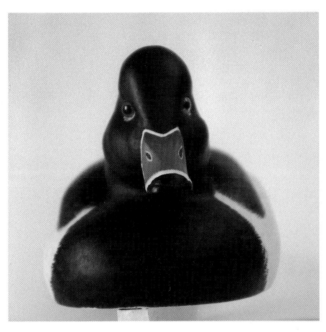

Front view.

Profile of finished gunning decoy.

Profile of finished decorative decoy.

215

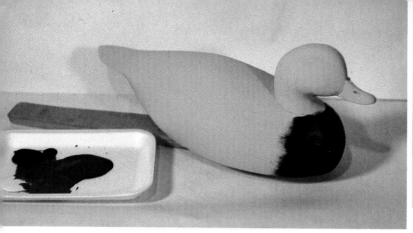

For the baldpate drake I have undercoated the breast with a mixture of Ronan burnt sienna, ultramarine blue and white. The burnt sienna is tinted with the blue to get a purplish red and it is lightened with the white. The same drake breast color can be mixed using red, blue, green, black, and white.

After the undercoat is dry I sand the entire decoy lightly and drill the eye holes with a brace and 5/16" bit. I use 7mm black eyes for all birds except those with red or yellow eyes. The black shows up better than brown after the decoys are in use for a while. Drilling with a brace and bit makes a neater hole and the bit doesn't "run" like a high speed bit will do. Putting the eyes in after priming means that I'll have to scrape paint off the eyes only once, after the final coat. Also, the holes drill more cleanly through the undercoated wood than through unprimed wood.

I next lay out the white patches on the sides extending back to the speculum and then paint in the green speculum. I paint in the black on the back tail and under the tail. I also paint a second coat of white on the bottom and all parts except the head that will be white on the completed bird.

Robert Biddle—Baldpate

Head: I mix raw umber to my white until I get a putty color, which I apply to the head.

I mix the final breast color of purplish-pink using burnt sienna, ultramarine blue and white to lighten and add some raw umber and white to the same mixture for the back. The sides are the same breast paint with yellow ochre and white added to get that rusty brown color.

Using a Windsor & Newton Series 995, ¾" flat sable (with a clear acrylic handle), I add white to both the breast and back color paints and add a series of feathering strokes only to break up the large areas of solid color.

I put the green patch around the eye with Ronan C.P. Green Medium, lightening the center with a little yellow ochre blended in.

I put black dots on the head with a Robert Simmons FT4 striping brush and run the dots closer together towards the rear of the head until its almost solid black on the back of the neck.

To complete the painting, I mix a brownish-gray and lay in the primaries as shown using the same striping brush. I then put the black line ahead and white line behind the speculum. I put in the black lines at the base of the bill where it meets the head, the nostrils, and end of bill. It's now finished except for scraping the paint off the eyes which I do with my fingernail.

Rigging the decoy: I use either a leather thong held on by a nail or a ring and staple for the anchor line. Care should be taken to assure that the nail or staple is set far enough forward to avoid going into the body cavity and possibly causing a leak sometime in the future.

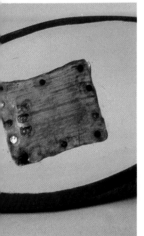

I use keels or bottom weights for my decoys depending on whether or not they're going to be used in rough water. The keel bird is much more stable, but is harder to transport with the added bulk. On this drake I've used a lead weight approximately 2" x 3" x ¼" thick that has been hammered to a bevel on the edge to make it less subject to becoming tangled.

To balance the decoy I put the weight on with a big rubber band and float it in a tub of water. I move the weight under the rubber band until the decoy sets just right in the water, then I carefully turn it over and nail the weight in place. I always check it again to make sure it is balanced perfectly before putting a line and anchor on it. It's now ready to go into the water.

Dan Brown—Green-Winged Teal
(Hen and drake)

DRAKE

Tertial area
Burnt umber and white

Primaries

Burnt umber edge with lighter hue

Burnt umber and white

Sides and back

Black

Thalo green with cadmium yellow

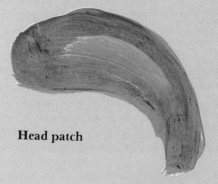

Head patch

Sides

Thalo green with cadmium yellow

Yellow ochre   Black   Raw umber   White

Head

Burnt sienna

218

Tertials and tail

Burnt umber and white

Burnt umber

Black

Thalo green

Secondaries and head patch

White

Cadmium yellow

Yellow ochre

Undertail

HEN

Black
burnt umber and white

Black

Burnt umber

Yellow ochre

Sides and chest

Back

Burnt umber

Black

Side feathers   Burnt umber

Bill   Purple

Back

Burnt umber and black

Thalo blue   Alizarin Crimson   Paynes gray and white   Thalo blue   **219**

Undercoat of black on side and foreback. Gray tertial area—head burnt sienna with cadmium yellow undercoat of green patch on head and secondaries for iridescent look

Drake—side and foreback black—tertial area gray. Head—burnt sienna—thalo green patch—black bill. Hen—crown and back burnt umber—sides and cheeks burnt umber mixed with white—secondaries thalo green on both

Hen, sides, cheek, and chest areas burnt umber mixed with white. Back and crown burnt umber—speculum undercoated with cadmium yellow

Finished drake—note yellow ochre band around green patch on head—and white crescent on side near shoulder area. Note yellow patch under tail (yellow ochre mixed with white)

Pair of finished teal. Note—chest color of drake—burnt sienna, yellow ochre and white with black spots

Finished hen decoy—note burnt umber eye line—chest and side feathers striped in with burnt umber and a much lighter hue (burnt umber mixed with white) same as on back. Also white trailing edge of speculum

The old and the new decoy on left was best of show winner in Michigan 20 years ago. Beside it still another winner today

The pair—

Teal hen—note the gray bill with hint of purple at base of bill near head

Teal drake—note the side and back area which was painted gray—(gesso and black mixed) over the black undercoat. This was then combed to create the vermiculations

Again the pair—a perfect temptation for the real thing

221

When painting a wooden decoy, seal with two coats of lacquer sanding sealer 50/50 with sealer and thinner.

Paint bottom half of brant with flat latex house paint (also any other area which may have a white undercoat).

Use hair dryer for quicker drying of water base paint—less chance of raising grain.

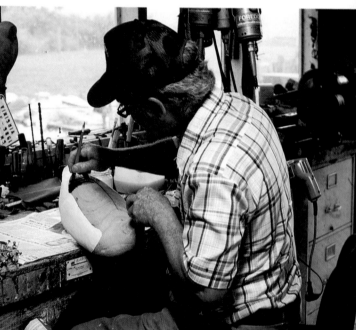

Tertials and tail black—upper tail coverts are white. "Cigar" feels you should show a lot of white on brant; these are good field marks.

Atlantic Brant

Be sure to keep side feathers forward, they do not come way back to tail.

Using bristle brush, paint white arcs on side, start at front and go toward tail.

With raw umber and white mixed (Cigar uses Aqua tec raw umber) arc through white on sides. If a softer effect is desired, use fan blender—all this has to be done wet on wet, so you must work quickly.

Blend raw umber and white arcs

On back feathers use raw umber and white for feather edges and paint interior darker.

Further feathering on back

Delbert "Cigar" Daisey

Paint head and breast black. Paint head and breast two or three coats.

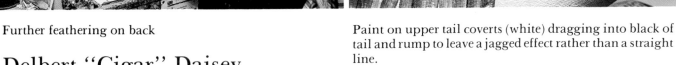

Paint on upper tail coverts (white) dragging into black of tail and rump to leave a jagged effect rather than a straight line.

Completed with eye set—white streaks only on sides of neck, go over several times as head will be used as a handle and paint could rub off.

Brants eye view of Brant decoy. Cigar just threw these
decoys out of his door into water outside his shop

Two cork brant made by Cigar in 1969 and 1971 in the
collection of Dan Brown

Paul's broadbill rig, garvy and layout boat.

Paul Dobrowski—Canvasback Hen

Pallet—blend light and dark pre-mixed colors to change values of base colors.

Apply dark values to feather groups. Go over with lighter values to overlay—back to front.

Application of successive coats of color detailing dark areas of feather groups.

Split feathers in rump area to meet back of side pocket.

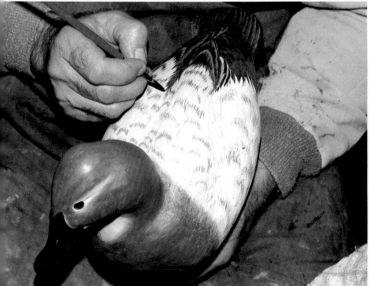

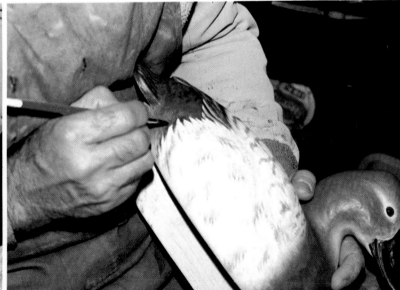

Detailing feather groups on back area.

Another view. Applying several shades or values of light over dark areas to create depth in feathers.

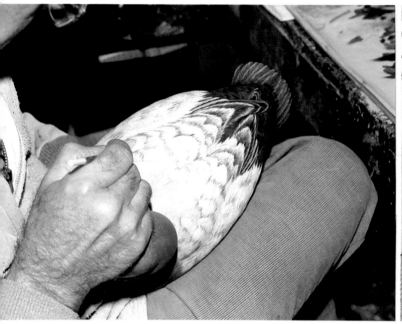

Applying light over dark to soften area.

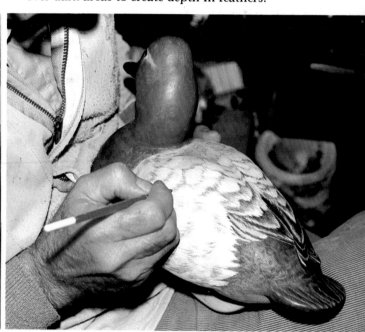

Another view.

Pallet—*Note:* Always stay with pre-mixed colors for various parts of bird.

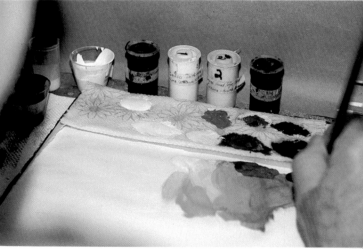

Pallet.

226

Applying darker values of chest color on the chest.

Color washing rump area.

Lightening eye area.

Lightening feather edges in rump area.

Detail breast area.

Feathering breast area.

227

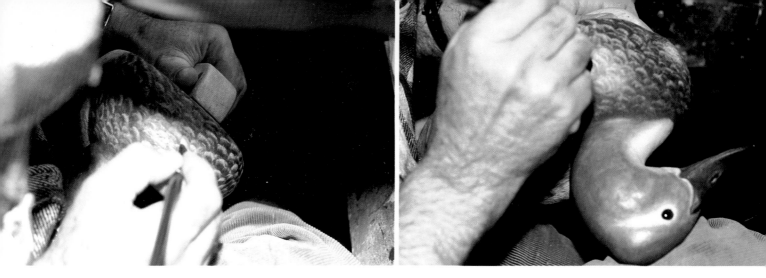

Breast feathering continued.

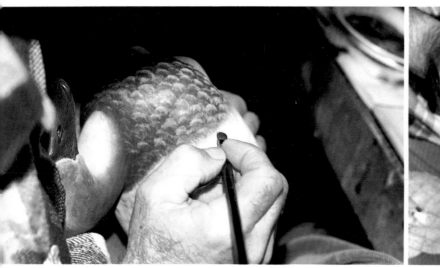

Lightening chest feather edges.

Paint chest up to neck area.

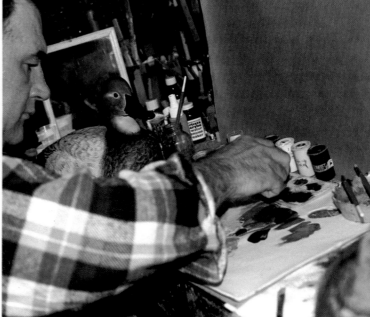

Mixing colors—stay with basic container colors.

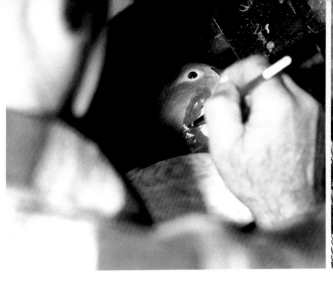

Paint another value of color on side of head.

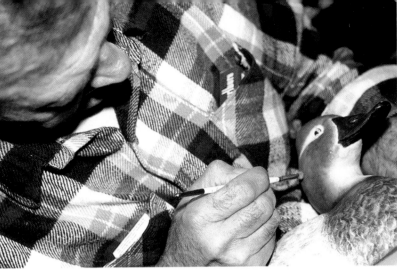

Stipple blend wet colors, dark-to-light, to soften edges.

Color wash tail area to tone down sharpness of light feather edges.

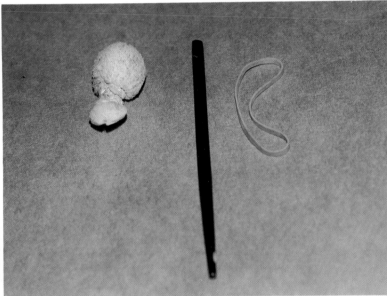

Vermiculation sponge, old paint brush handle and rubber band.

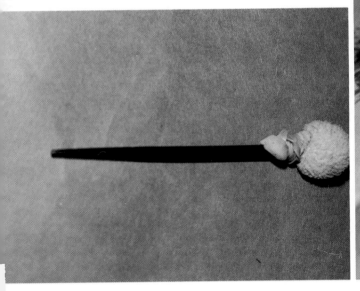

Cosmetic sponge edges to be used for vermiculations.

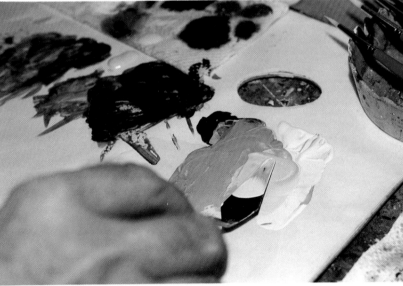

Several values of colors for vermiculations.

229

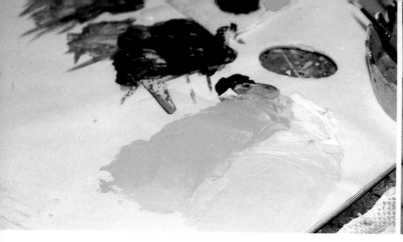

Vermiculation colors must be spread out like printer's ink so sponge does not pick up too much paint.

Select bare minimum of paint on sponge and stamp on various feather groups.

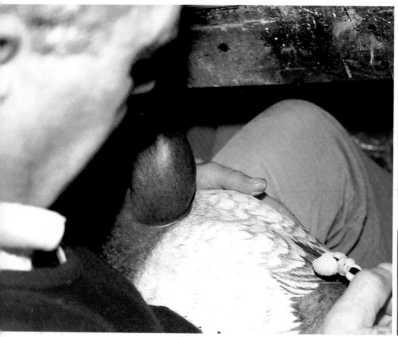

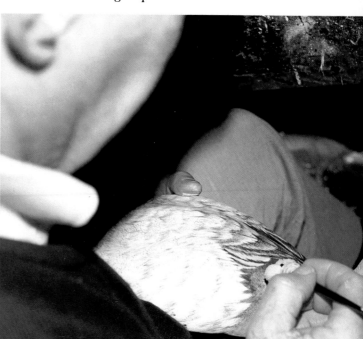

Application of vermiculations on tertial feathers.

Vermiculation continued.

Vermiculation continued.

230

Various values of color to finish painting head.

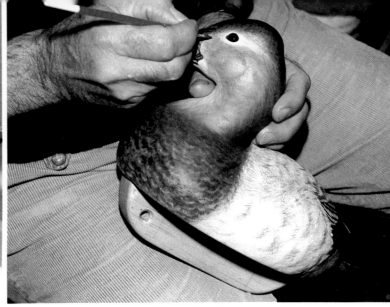

Finishing head using pointillism painting technique.

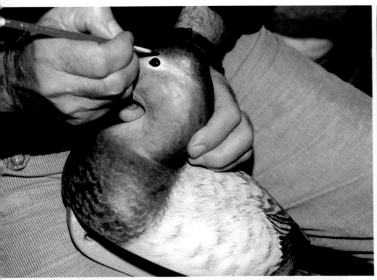

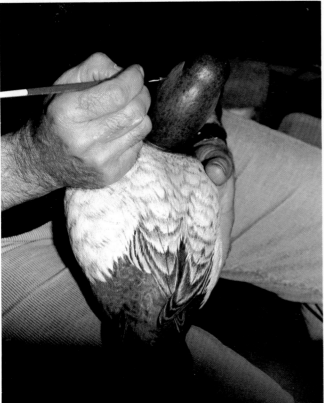

Pointillism continued on head areas.

Acrylic matt varnish mixed with warm black and burnt umber for painting bill.

231

Acrylic matt varnish mixed with warm black and burnt umber for painting bill.

Painting bill.

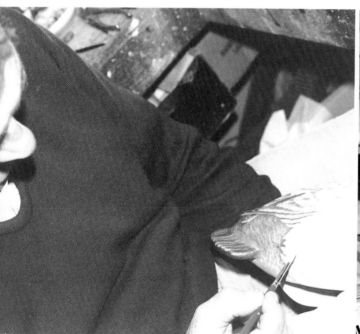

Finishing touches to side pocket edges.

Finished bird.

1st Best of Show 1986. Pacific Southwest Wildfowl Arts, Inc. California Open, Service Class—Gunning Decoy.

Finished bird.

Oil base Valspar goose brown on back.

Sides and chest painted with gray (Use black, white and brown to make gray).

Harold Haman—Canada Goose

Paint head with rustoleum flat black.

Paint under rump with white.

233

Paint rump and tail black (Rustoleum flat black).

Use fan brush with gray to put feathering shapes on back (Note: Just touch edge of brush to make feather edge.)

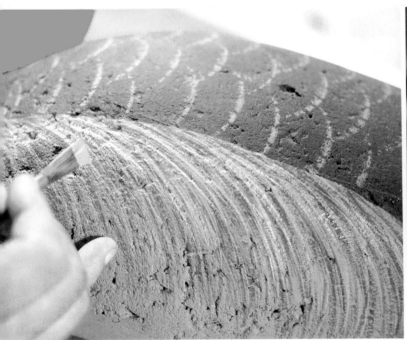

Use flat brush to make lighter gray and brown streaks on sides.

Paint white patch on head.

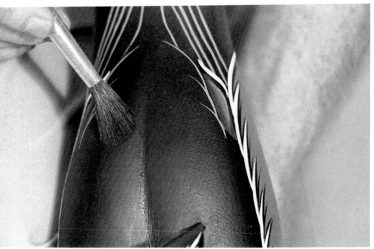

Prime with Binns white outside oil paint. When dry sand lightly. All colors are artists oil.

Back is painted with combination of black and permanent green.

Sides are painted yellow ochre mixed with raw umber.

Charlie "Speed" Joiner —Wood Duck

White blended along bottom edge.

Stipple blended.

Under rump bottom half white, upper half black.

Brush marks dragged from black to white creating a feathered look.

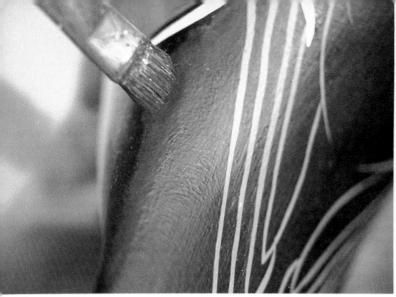

Burnt sienna blended just forward of tail.

Head color is permanent green.

Prussian blue blended on lower parts.

White patch.

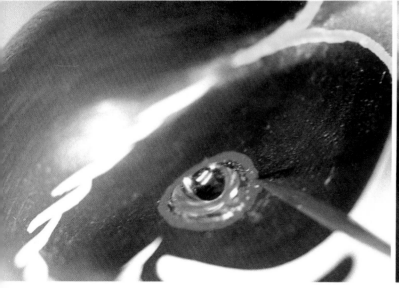

Cadmium red eye ring.

White streaks on crown.

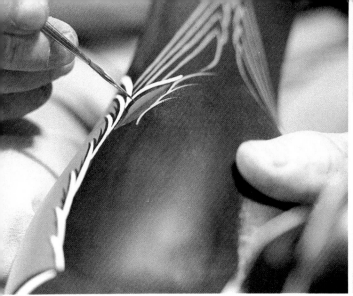

Speculum prussian blue and white.

White stripes behind and above speculum.

Off white primaries.

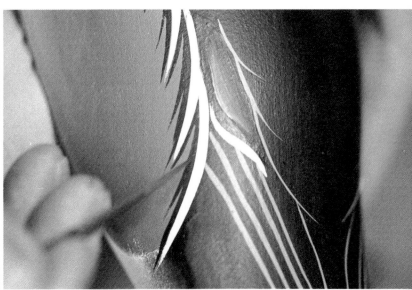

White and black stripes (crescent on sides).

Black patch on side.

White patch on side.

Red and white blended, then black ridge and nail.

Red and white blended, then black ridge and nail.

Cadmium yellow outline on bill adjacent to head.

White spots on chest.

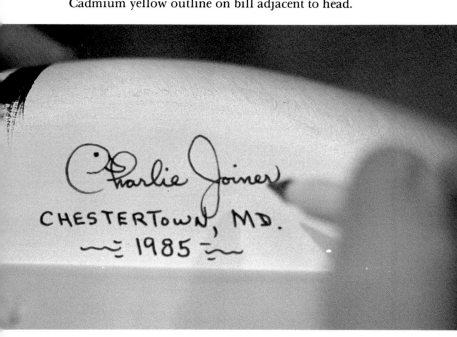

Charlie Joiner
CHESTERTOWN, MD.
1985

The famous Joiner signature.

238

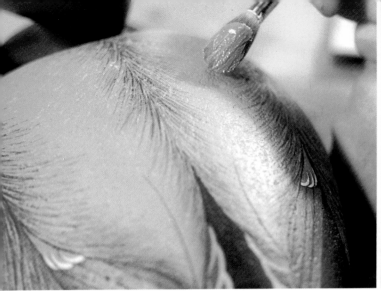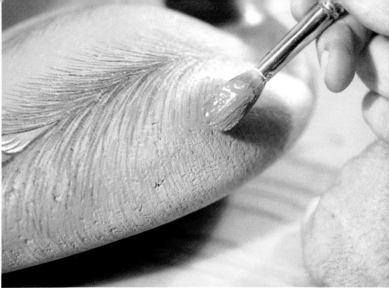

Body—Paint the entire body grey. A little added raw umber will "soften" the mixture of black and white.

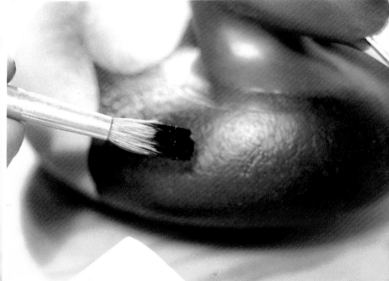

Tail—Black-here the dark area is extended over the flanks and rump, indicating the tertials.

Breast—Black-a line can be followed here to indicate the shoulders.

Head—Reddish brown, mix red, raw umber, a little purple and just a touch of yellow. Crown and temples may be darkened with more raw umber.

Ned Mayne— Red Head

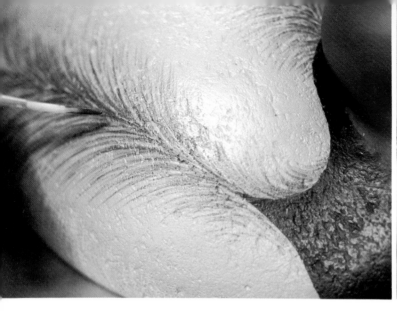

Vermiculation—Thinned down black-applied in lots of quick, little wispy strokes along the back and sides. (Doesn't take long at all.)

Primaries—Medium brownish-grey. Here, some left-over body color can be mixed with a little more black and a good deal more raw umber. I usually define the leading edges with a black line and the trailing edges with "off" white.

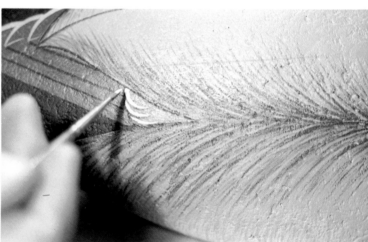

Outlining the primaries with gray

Outlining the secondaries with white

Finishing Touches—Tailfeathers are indicated by a single stroke with paint left over from the primaries. Speculum is rendered by a few strokes of light grey and white.
*Note: The omission of a priming or sealing step is intentional. Because of the resin used as a binder, decoys made of "wiley" cork simply don't require it. Heads and keels should probably get two coats of paint however.

Bill—light bluish-grey, add small amount of blue to black and white. By painting the bill first a larger brush can be used, eliminating marks and streaks.

Take raw umber and make a thin wash. Apply this wash to the vermiculated area.

Mix black into burnt umber and apply to the back of the head as a base coat. Now stipple black into the base coat.

The head will require three shades of brown. To achieve this, apply burnt umber to the top and backside of the head, raw umber to the middle and raw umber with a dab

You may mix some red metallic flakes into the paint and apply it to the upper rear side of the head. This is best accomplished when the paint is still wet.

of white to the front. Now simply blend the colors together by stippling and lightly brushing.

Paint the bill light gray with a small amount of ultramarine blue. Detail the bill with black.

Terry McNulty—Pintail   241

Additional feather groups may be added if desired. Take black and apply with a 00 Kats Tongue Langnickel Brush. You may then soften the feathers with a wash of raw umber.

Authors note: With every stroke of the brush, the bird comes more alive and you think of the ducks that will stool to it. As I have said many times in the past, if there is anything that I would give extra attention to, it is the head.

Apply black to all the tertial feathers. You may mix a little green irridescent powder to the black for a more authentic look, but be careful not to overdue the irridescence.

Using a little raw umber with lambswool in it, paint the primaries. While they are still wet, take some thin lambswool on the tip of the brush, place the brush on the edge of the feather and draw back through. Clean your

Apply white to both edges of the feathers, making the outside of the feather edge twice as wide as the inside edge.

brush, dampen it and with the paint still wet, draw lightly through as to muddle it. Now tip the edge of the feathers with lambswool.

Using a Langnickel 5954 and gray paint, work from the shaft outward and towards the rear of the feather, drawing your brush evenly creating feather barbs.

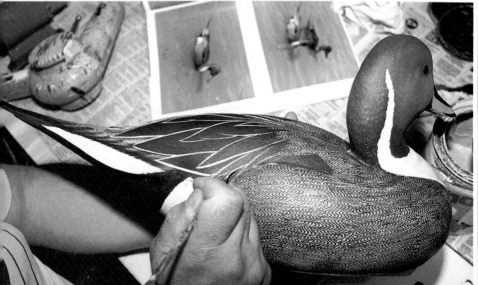

Using your black, straighten the edges nearest the shaft.

With a thin wash of raw umber, wash the back of the decoy.

Redefine the outer edge of the tertial feathers with white. Feather splits may be added for more realism.

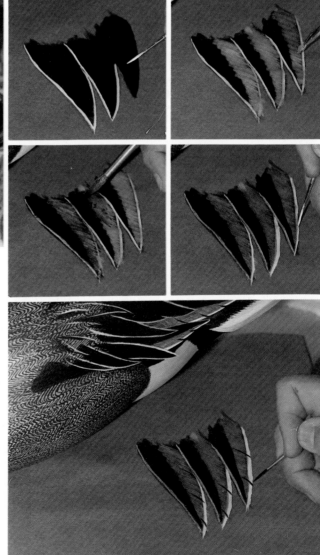

Paint the tail with black and green metallic flakes.

These steps have been discussed in Fig. 63 thru 69.

The painting on a hunting decoy should be flat and not shine. Note the soft appearance this decoy has.

Paint the rump white and stipple yellow ochre into the wet paint.

Cut in feather edges with white and a small brush.

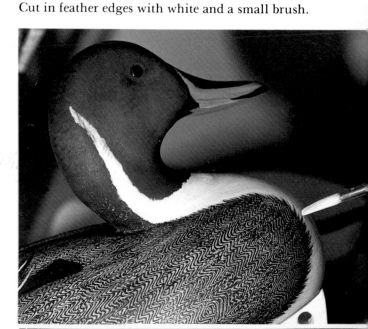

The upper tail coverts may be painted gray. While the paint is wet, stipple in or make small feathers with raw umber. Dry with a hair dryer and give this area a thin wash of raw umber.

Paint the chest with white. Feathers may be added by stippling raw umber into the wet paint.

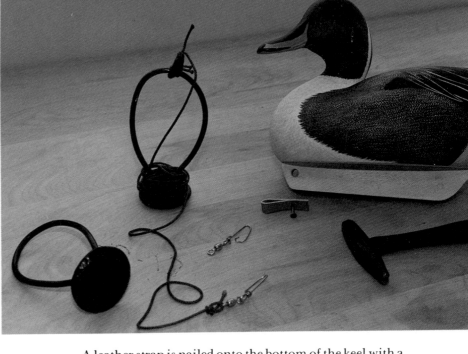

Edge some of the chest feathers with white.

A leather strap is nailed onto the bottom of the keel with a monel brad. The hole in the keel is for emergencies. In case the leather breaks or the nail pulls out, you may put the line through the hole and use the decoy for the balance of the day. The snap swivels are very convenient as they can be detached easily and also help eliminate knots. The mushroom anchor with a coated plastic wire loop is handy to slip over your decoy's head without scratching it. Also the lead may be dipped in Plasti-Dip, which comes in Red or green. You may mix the two together and you will get an olive drab. This rubber coating will help protect your stools.

Note the shading in the head.

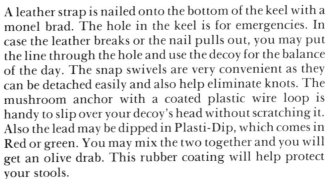

Let's go hunting!

A good decoy will have style and appeal from any angle.

245

Ralph Nocerino—Black Duck

Best of show "shooting stool".

Head crown—burnt umber. Eye line—burnt umber. Cheek and neck—burnt umber. Raw sienna and white mixed to make light face color streaks of burnt umber. Bill color—yellow ochre mixed with black to make an olive green. Body color—burnt umber mixed with tiny amount of ultramarine blue.

Finished carvings.

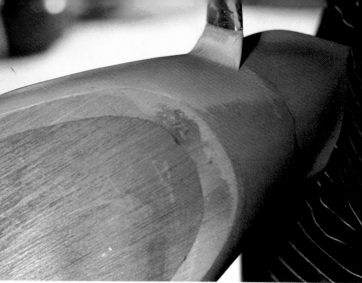

Mix black, white and burnt umber to make light gray.

Paint back and sides.

Repeat gray coat while it is wet, paint center of back and side pocket areas with burnt umber and blend colors.

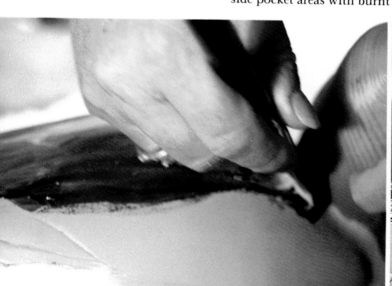

Repeat gray coat while it is wet, paint center of back and side pocket areas with burnt umber and blend colors.

Blending umber into gray.

William Veasey—Mallard

Final blending.

Black under rump.

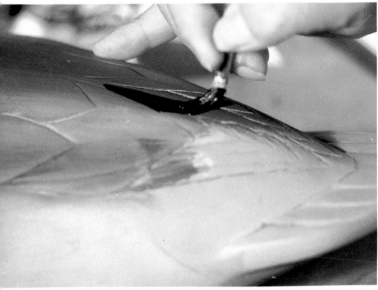

Black upper rump.

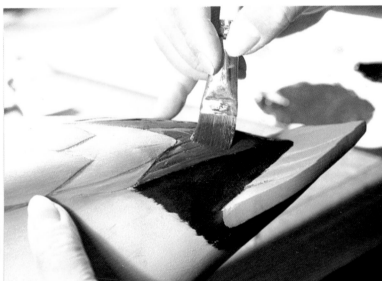

Primaries burnt umber.

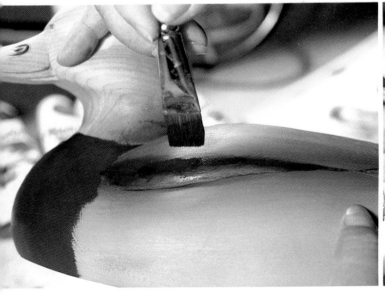

Reinforce burnt umber along side pockets.

Equal amounts of burnt sienna and burnt umber for chest color.

Highlighting tail feathers with white.

White band between black and gray areas under rump.

Ultramarine blue on secondaries or speculum.

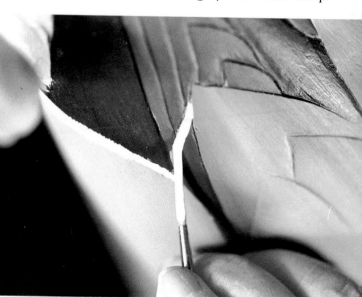

Trailing edge of white on secondaries.

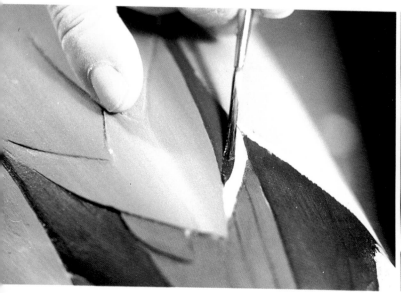

Black strip adjacent to trailing edge of white on secondaries.

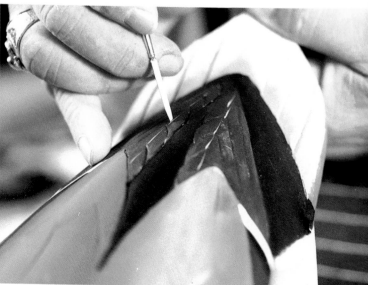

Highlighting quill on primaries.

250

Undercoat head with Thalo green.

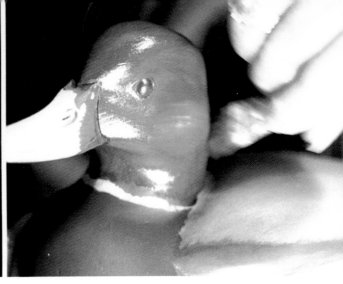

Blend yellow green into cheek area (wet on wet).

Blend black into crown and down back of neck (wet on wet).

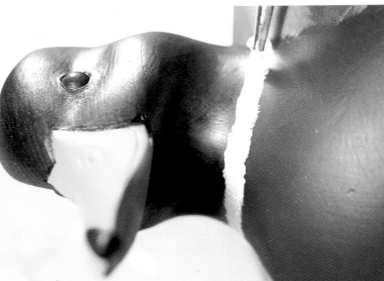

Paint white ring around neck leaving 1'' gap behind head.

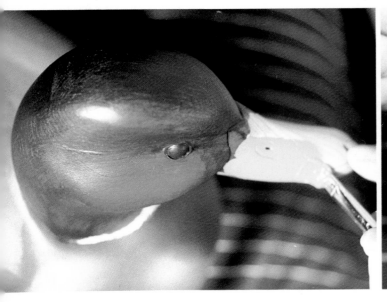

Bill yellow ochre.

Nail painted black.

Stirring the primer.

Priming decoy with Kilz-primer and stain killer (this primer will eliminate sap bleeding through the paint).

Painting tail area with black rustoleum.

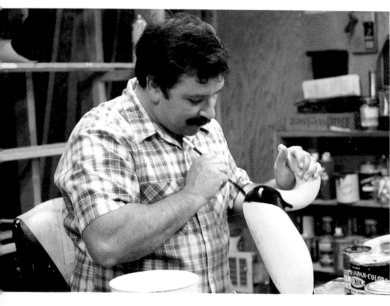

Painting breast area with black rustoleum.

Black under coat on head.

252 Gilmore ''Butch'' Waggoner—Upper Bay Canvasback

Feathering by using stiff brush which has been cut down so that when applied to decoy it will slightly arc creating a rounded feather edge.

Painting bill flat black.

(Author's note: All back feathering of the Havre de Grace style has the feathers running backwards—this was created for ease in painting and does make a nice effect).

Applying "tail" feathers.

(Author's note: In the Havre de Grace style the primary or wing feathers are always referred to as "tail" feathers.

Refining the "tail" feathers.

Painting head with burnt sienna and raw umber and some black blended into crown and forecheek.

Painting eye with an eyer (this is a local term, it is a wooden tube) eye is red with black center.

Finished decoy.

Havre de Grace style goose by Charlie Joiner.

R. Madison Mitchell black duck. Note feather pattern done by using nail to scratch patterns onto decoy.

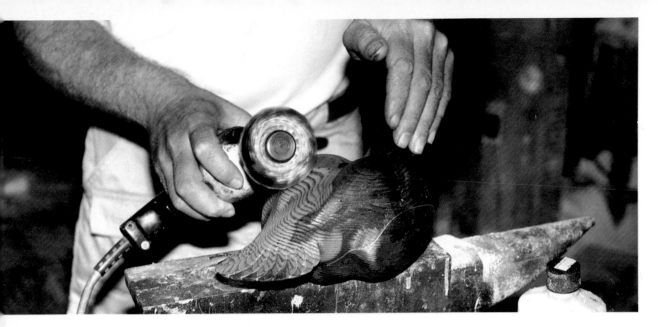

Clean char off torched bird with cloth wheel, then seal with 50/50 alcohol and white shellac.

Harry J. Waite—Bufflehead

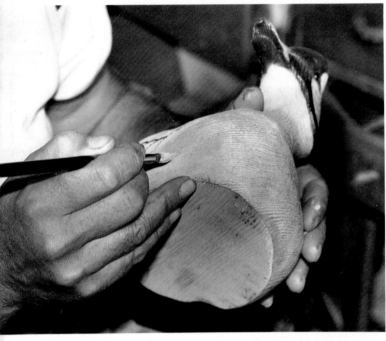

Use white oil paint for chest and sides (all paints are artists oils).

White patch on head.

Black paint on back and tail.

Scraping paint off eye.

Wipe paint off with tissue.

Thalo green on head.

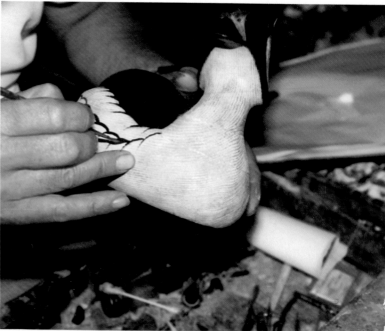

Black feather strips.

Blue gray on bill (paynes gray and white mixed), paint nail black.

*Note: all paint is wiped so that grain and brown from torching shows through.

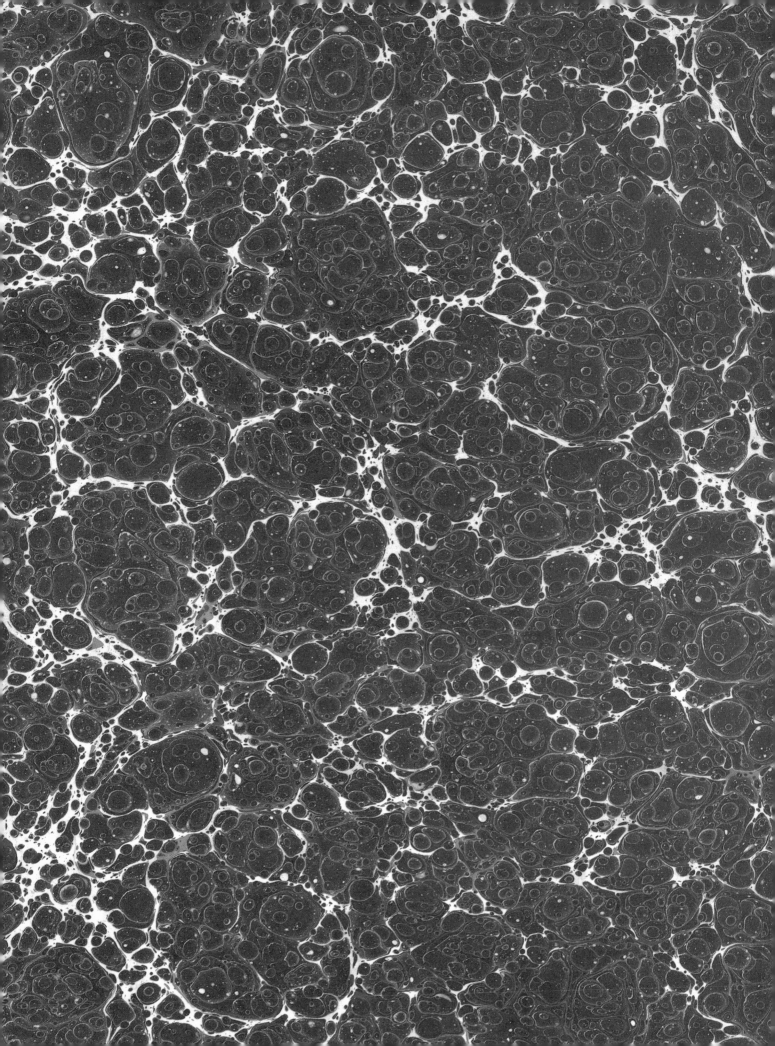